G000065961

RENAISSANCE TRIATHLETE

RENAISSANCE TRIATHLETE

Enjoying Sport as an Older Athlete
Managing Mind and Body

DOUGLAS WOOD

First edition

This paperback edition published in 2020

 First published by
HULLO CREATIVE LTD.
www.hullocreative.com

Copyright © Douglas Wood 2020

All rights reserved. No portion of this book may be reproduced, stored in a retrieval system, or transmitted in any form or by any means, (mechanical, electronic, photocopying, recording, or otherwise), without written permission from the copyright owner and publisher.

Cover images

Bratislava 2017: Halfway in the swim - the beach exit and re-entry
Photo © Chris Wood

On the bike course at Strathclyde Park 2018
Photo © Ian Vatter

ISBN 978-0-9935366-8-7

For
Chris
and
Johanne, Kirsten & Ross

Contents

Foreword
by Alistair Brownlee

I've been lucky enough to be involved in endurance sport for most of my life. For the better part of this time it has been a way of life and I'd love for it to stay as such for many years to come. The physical and psychological benefits of living an active lifestyle are there for all to see. It's easy to lose the love of activity at times, especially when it gets tougher to get out of the door. But like crossing the threshold as you leave the house on a cold evening, those first steps are the hardest, they need all the encouragement they can get and are rarely regretted later.

Renaissance Triathlete is an enjoyable, fascinating and important piece of work. It's both educational and motivational for the older athlete. I urge everyone to read it and be encouraged to be active - especially in the form of Triathlon! It is an honour and a pleasure to write this foreword. I hope it helps me stay active for many years to come and has the same effect on you.

Happy reading

Alistair

One
INTRODUCTION

In the early hours of 19th August 2008 I crept upstairs in the middle of the night to watch the men's triathlon at the Beijing Olympics. Viewing highlights afterwards, when the result is known, is no substitute for watching the full race live.

With the sound turned low so as not to disturb the rest of the house, I watched events unfold. There were no break-aways in the early part of the race so it was going to come down to the 10km run to sort out the final places. As the run progressed, the Canadian Simon Whitfield, Olympic champion from eight years before, developed a small lead and was looking most likely to win.

Then suddenly I became aware of excitement in the commentator's voice, saying that Frodeno of Germany was coming through with a late charge. It was the first time I'd heard his name mentioned. The camera homed in closer to the action; it was Jan, my pal Jan, who had been sitting next to me on the plane to Hamburg less than twelve months before. I'd forgotten that he would be in the race.

In the final 200m or so, Frodeno surged through from fourth or fifth place to win the gold medal. So there I was, jumping out of my chair trying not to make a noise and with no one to share the moment. The only person who could appreciate what had happened would be Andy, my travelling partner from the same Hamburg trip. I sent him a text message - was he watching? Yes, he was!

It was a pivotal moment. I felt part of it; no longer on the outside. Participating in sport had drawn me into its wider family.

I was always keen on running and developed this interest further when I was a student at university in the mid 1960s. This was a time when people would hang up their boots when they reached 30. Cross country, hill running, orienteering, track and road races; running was my sport.

At that time it was unusual to find older people still involved, unless they were officials. But without realising it, I was at the start of a new generation - the baby boomers born in 1946 immediately after the Second World War. Unlike the generation before us, we didn't stop when we reached a certain age. We enjoyed our sport and continued doing it for as long as we could.

Slowly, sport and attitudes to sport began to change.

Veteran categories were introduced for the over 35s and over time a whole structure of age group categories developed across many sports.

By the mid 1970s going out for a run started to become socially acceptable, no longer an odd thing to do. And at the same time a new concept was born: the running shoe.

This was the beginning of the jogging boom. Those without an athletic background started running for recreational fitness. Fred Lebow founded the People's Marathon in New York, which in turn inspired the creation of a similar celebration of running in the UK. And I was among the participants in that very first London Marathon in 1981.

Even then I thought, why would you ever want to stop running?

I never thought I'd be running at 70 - but I never believed I couldn't. Such thoughts simply hadn't occurred to me. But here I am, the age of 70 came and went four years ago. And I'm not just running, but swimming, cycling and competing in triathlons.

As you get older you can't avoid slowing down, but you can influence the rate at which the slowing occurs.

It's about how you adapt with age. Learning how to get the best out of your changing capabilities. There is enormous satisfaction to be gained from discovering what's possible, even now. And I feel I am always learning more about the relationship between fitness, effort and performance.

Participation in sport leads me to places I wouldn't normally have cause to visit and into the paths of those I wouldn't otherwise come across. At a time of life when the natural trend is for the funnel to narrow, sport keeps me in touch with the bigger picture.

When sport has been a significant part of your life, you want to enjoy it for as long as you can.

This book is a reflection of my experiences as an older athlete, after four seasons of triathlons in my 70s. It addresses the physical and mental challenges encountered through ageing, dealing with setbacks and compensating for slowing down in some areas by making improvements in others.

My account is set in the context of triathlon, with the core elements of swimming, cycling and running.

This is not a coaching or a training manual. The focus is on movement, agility and skills - on being smarter, getting the best out of yourself and achieving the best possible outcome in the context of your circumstances and aspirations. Always searching for the ideal blend of physical effort and mental application.

Sometimes it's better not to be influenced by the science. Research studies suggest that age-related decline in performance in sport follows a downward curve, a trajectory that becomes more pronounced around the age of 60 before decreasing exponentially beyond the age of 70. And the rapid rate of decline by the age of 70 appears to be a common feature in all sports.

I'm glad that no one told me this. We're all different. There can be an average but no one is the average person. I took control and managed the shape of my own graph.

The following chapters journey through triathlon, reflecting on the physical and mental challenges for the older athlete, while giving a flavour of the essence of the sport. The appendices include a summary of research findings relating to ageing in sport (Appendix 2), specifically age-related decline in performance for triathlon and for the sports that make up triathlon.

The issues will be relevant to many disciplines. But most of all, this book is a celebration of the enjoyment of sport. And I hope that you may be encouraged to keep going, look forward and plan ahead.

Two

AN EIGHTH DECADE

It's my 70th birthday and we're in France. Our visit coincides with the Euro 2016 football tournament so there's quite a lot going on. I don't know anything about Châteauroux but, two hours south of Paris by train, it proves to be a town full of history and character.

I have been looking forward to this for some time. It's the European aquathlon championships, a swim-run (the branch of triathlon that doesn't have a cycling element) and needless to say I'm a first-timer in the 70-74 age category.

There are fewer participants in the aquathlon than at corresponding European triathlon championships, not more than 300. And it's disappointing to find only two of us in the M70-74 category. The other is Mike, the best in the world for his age at triathlon and he just happens to be the same age as I am. He is a good friend, a benchmark rather than an opponent.

Starting in the late afternoon, the race consists of a 1km swim followed by a 5km run in calm conditions. We swim in a scenic lake set in parkland on the edge of the town. Rather quaintly, the lake is on an island, an eyot, in the River Indre. The water is warm, too warm for wetsuits to be allowed. While I might consider myself a competent swimmer, I am some way short of being a strong swimmer. However, you have to take it as you find it.

They say it's the same for everyone, but of course it's not. The extra buoyancy provided by a wetsuit is of greater assistance to weaker swimmers. Realising there would be few, if any, weaker swimmers in a championship aquathlon, I am concerned not to find myself cast adrift.

I try to start quickly. But those I try to keep pace with just move away. Fortunately I can see a few green swim hats over to my right so I head that way and manage to cling on to them in a small group. It looks as though we are the tail of the bunch - but at least we're not detached.

Then, turning at the first buoy, I'm reassured to see there are still others behind us. So I settle down and focus on keeping in touch. By the beach exit at 600m I am in a group of three. The exit seems to be a feature for the entertainment of spectators - we all clamber out of the water to run round a flag and go right back in again. Staying with the other two, I keep a steady rhythm for the final 400m to the swim exit, pleased to have managed a non-wetsuit swim without making an exhibition of myself. Though close to the back of the field, my swim was much better than I would have been capable of a few years before.

At the transition area I take some additional time to put on a calf guard. Better to take the precaution than risk a muscle injury - which is exactly what happened in similar circumstances at Geneva the year before. It possibly takes me an extra 10 to 12 seconds to fit the tight sleeve over my wet leg, but it's certainly worthwhile. After all, it is important to finish.

In the absence of a cycling component my legs feel fresher than at the start of a triathlon run and I am enjoying it. It always takes a little time to find your running rhythm when following on from a different activity, but once settled, I close the gap to a Frenchman who had left the transition area ahead of me. From there we stay together until we reach the blue carpet heralding the final 100m or so to the finish banner.

It is an exaggeration to suggest we sprint the final 50m but it feels as though we do. The sensation brings back some good memories. We can tell from our respective body markings that we're in different age categories, but nevertheless it feels exhilarating to have been 'racing'.

So although there are only two competitors in my age group, I have still had the thrill of racing against others. I declare it a best race possible (BRP) and still maintain it was definitely the most enjoyable way to spend my 70th birthday.

I did note a couple of things that could have been better. I lost a few seconds in transition when putting on a calf sleeve, though it was a wise precaution in the circumstances and I wouldn't have done anything differently. More pertinently though, I could have saved a few seconds by grabbing my number belt and fastening it round my waist while on the run, rather than putting it on before getting into my shoes. A thought to tuck away for next time.

I had mixed feelings about winning a silver medal in a two-person contest. Mike finished well ahead of me. But I am satisfied that it is a worthy performance. My 5km run split was better than usual and, after all, it was my birthday. I never imagined I would be able to do that sort of thing when I turned 70.

In my late 60s the thought of doing a triathlon when I was 70 became quite appealing, a kind of subconscious target. When the time came in 2016, I took part in eight triathlons and two aquathlons, all in a single year.

The journey up to that point was a bumpy ride but once I reached the territory beyond, things seemed to be calmer, as though I'd gone through the sound barrier. The horizon lifted, a bigger picture unfolded and I continued without an end point in mind. I would keep going while able to do so. For as long as I could enjoy it.

How do I feel? Has anything changed? Am I doing things differently? Generally... I feel good.

Over four seasons in my 70s I've taken part in 34 triathlons and 9 aquathlons in the UK, Europe and beyond. Change has been gradual and some changes have been enhancing. I've found it important to learn and to keep learning. If I am going to continue to enjoy sport I need to train and race smarter, not harder.

Preparation and planning is still crucial. A casual approach is likely to lead to an unsatisfactory outcome. To enjoy sport, I need to take it seriously.

In 2016 I made progress with achieving 'flow' in my races, avoiding high effort levels and letting this pervade my racing mindset to advantage. That year too my swimming was more consistent, beginning to shift from a weakness to a strength and I felt greater confidence in non-wetsuit situations.

I was enjoying the calf sleeves (or guards) that I started using in mid season 2015. They made a significant difference to my running, providing support for the muscles that allowed me to train more consistently.

I am conscious of the effects of ageing. And I am conscious these changes may accelerate with increasing age. It's an inescapable trend but this trajectory can give rise to opportunities. I have to make do with less strength and agility but some aspects of my performances have improved: my technique, my efficiency of movement and my general performance 'know how'. And this is what brings me enjoyment.

I have learned not to compare myself with others or with my past achievements. That is the route to frustration and disappointment. Instead I think about how I can have the best race possible - the BRP - in each prevailing context. Achieving that - that is what brings satisfaction.

We all have limitations, real and imaginary. Those that are always present have to be managed. In deference to my past history I do not run up steep gradients and I avoid hard surfaces. And I will always be careful when applying a lot of pressure through the bike pedals.

Although run courses in a triathlon are invariably on unyielding surfaces, I will normally cope with the 5km for a sprint triathlon when required. However I rule out any running course longer than that, such as the 'standard' triathlon, unless most of the running is off-road. That's just down to the particular legacy of my accumulated wear and tear.

With other limitations you cannot be certain if they are real or imagined. Many come under the category I call PEN syndrome - the 'pre-event niggles' that surface before an event and gnaw away at your confidence.

Often it's the same issue. My ankle - the 'good' one - becomes very sore for no apparent reason. It won't take my full weight. Or sometimes it's a knee or a calf muscle, or a combination of all these things. They emerge some days before an event, apparently from nowhere and can make me seriously consider withdrawing from a race.

But I usually decide to start anyway. I know that once I become engrossed in the race, I'll realise that the problems have disappeared.

I have learned to regard these niggles as my friends. Now I recognise them and am comforted by their arrival as a sign that I am ready and in the right place. I don't need to fight against them. They will help to enhance my performance on the day. Since I adopted this strategy, the PEN syndrome now appears to occur less often.

Sometimes a niggle can linger for weeks and hinder my training. But the race itself seems to have a cleansing effect for both the mind and body. I've thought about how I can achieve this sensation by introducing 'racing' mode into my training but it doesn't work. There's no substitute for a race.

The only way I've found around it is to join a 5km parkrun on Saturday mornings. Though a parkrun is not a race - it's a run - it seems to provide the necessary cleansing. And because it's regular it doesn't attract its own pre-event niggles like the prospect of a race does. Also, it helps me to stay familiar with the tempo and rhythm of the 5km distance run in a sprint triathlon. Overall it provides a very useful element of my training.

There are other limitations that affect the mind more than the body. Goals and aspirations, confidence, belief in yourself, the effect of belief that others may have in you - they all come into play. I will touch more on this later.

External factors can also have an influence. Whether circumstantial, environmental (e.g. location, weather conditions, the nature of the course), your state of fitness and health and where it all fits with your other priorities in life.

Considering all your potential limitations - real, imagined or unavoidable - it is only you who understand the full context in which you perform.

Personal satisfaction comes not from an absolute performance but from how you know you performed in the prevailing context. And that doesn't need to involve anyone else. You are doing this for your own pleasure.

Injury and illness are no fun at all. So look after yourself.

Three
TRIATHLON - THE SPORT

Triathlon is swimming, cycling and running. In that order. Many come to their first triathlon with a background in one of the three sports. Part of the enjoyment is gaining proficiency in the other two.

As the sport developed it branched out into a variety of forms that now come under the general umbrella of "multisport". So we have duathlon (cycling and running), aquathlon (swimming and running) and aquabike (swimming and cycling).

I am addressing triathlon in this book and occasionally aquathlon, which I started to become involved in when I was 69, after feeling I had become a stronger swimmer - primarily through improving swimming technique rather than fitness.

Swimming

Swimming is the obstacle that often stops people from taking the triathlon plunge. Cycling would be fine, and running, but not the swim.

But although there is a big difference between a strong swimmer and a weaker swimmer, the same applies for cycling and for running. In some ways swimming is the least significant element of a triathlon. Even a slower swimmer is likely to spend less time in the water than running or cycling. Something to bear in mind if the thought of front crawl is holding you back.

However, swimming is highly technical. Because speed is affected by the resistance of the water, the swimmer must find a streamlined body position - as horizontal as possible, presenting minimal surface area at their front. Body rotation in good swimming technique reduces water resistance by presenting a narrower front during each stroke. Remember too that the water doesn't move; it is the swimmer who moves, catching the water and using it to propel the body forward.

For years there were relatively few events in Scotland with open-water swims. Instead I entered events with indoor pool swims, five swimmers in a single lane, starting five seconds apart, up one side and back down the other. Overtaking was only permitted at the end of a length. For the remainder of the race you could never be sure whether another competitor had started a few seconds earlier or later than you.

At the start of the 2006 season, determined to take part in events with open-water swims, I finally acquired a wet-suit. It was a tip-off from club-mate Hans. The London Triathlon event had an offer hiring wetsuits for the season. Afterwards you could pay a modest balance and keep it, regardless of whether you were actually intending to do the London Triathlon. It was a good quality Orca suit with London Triathlon branding. I didn't know much about wet-suits but right away I liked it and had several years of good use from it.

A wetsuit doesn't just provide insulation in colder water, it also gives you crucial buoyancy. This makes a consider-able difference for weaker swimmers because it pushes them into the much sought after horizontal body position. It's like lying on a surfboard. Initially, for me the wetsuit could make a difference of nearly two minutes for the sprint distance swim of 750m, while also requiring less effort. The wetsuit is a leveller, not welcomed by better swimmers for whom it makes much less of a difference.

Competition rules do not permit the use of wetsuits if the water temperature exceeds a certain level (usually 22°C), rarely a risk in Scotland. But further south and especially abroad, the temperature threshold can come into play and if the situation is marginal, a final decision might not be announced until shortly before the start. This adds to pre-race anxiety levels, not only amongst those hoping to benefit from wetsuits but also amongst stronger swimmers who would much prefer a non-wetsuit swim to be declared.

I acquired my second wetsuit in 2011, a Blue Seventy Axis. The Axis had thicker sections in key places and special panels on the arms, all of which were supposed to be performance enhancing for swimmers at an intermediate level. It was certainly buoyant, but also bulkier and it did not roll up as neatly as the Orca I had always been so pleased with.

Six years later I relegated my Axis to be my training wetsuit and switched to a Zone 3 wetsuit. The Zone 3 made a special feature of the cuffs and ankles, designed to aid quick removal, an issue that had become important for me. The wetsuit performed well and I preferred it to the Axis.

There are so many wetsuits on the market it is difficult to decide what will be best. The descriptions of their distinctive features are rarely more helpful than those on a bottle of wine. I find it's best to talk to people about their experiences.

When I started to swim in open water I realised... this is what triathlon is all about. Demanding a completely different skill set, open water feels like the real thing.

Open water swims can have a dry or a wet start. For a dry start competitors simply line up on the shore and run into the water. But a wet start can take one of two forms: in the shallows, pushing off from the side of a pontoon or jetty; or away from the shore, lining up and treading water between a couple of buoys like boats in a regatta. Unless it is a race for elite competitors, there are no diving starts.

A massed start can be crowded but with experience you learn how to handle that and make use of other swimmers. In a swimming pool you become aware of a strong slipstream when swimming closely behind someone, making it possible to keep up with a faster swimmer. The same effect can occur in open water but there is another dimension added by the space and water conditions.

You can benefit from swimming alongside another swimmer, or by positioning yourself in the 'pocket' that forms between and behind two swimmers who are side by side. But the water conditions can complicate matters. If the water is clear you can see the feet in front and swimmers to the side, but when the water is cloudy or choppy it is easy to lose sight of others. And you must be sure that the person in front is not leading you away from the direct line.

You come to appreciate that the shallower the water, the warmer it is likely to be. Also, courses with shorter distances between the buoys present fewer navigational issues but can feel more crowded, because all the swimmers converge on the buoys frequently.

Finally, always remember to lift your goggles up off your face as soon as you come out of the water; otherwise you won't see clearly where you're treading. In bare feet that can be painful!

To anyone who is on the fence about triathlon because you doubt your swimming ability, I would say, give it a try. You might possibly surprise yourself.

Cycling

Most people know how to ride a bike so I won't linger here long. But cycling is arguably the most important part of a triathlon, taking roughly the same amount of time as the swim and run combined.

There are a host of rules, giving plenty of scope for infringements to incur penalties. The most common infringements relate to fastening of helmets, bike mounting and dismounting and drafting - the act of riding in the area of lower wind resistance behind another cyclist - of which the latter is the most contentious.

Elite races are normally draft legal - in other words, drafting is permitted. Riders can cycle in groups and the swim takes on a different significance, influencing whether you get into a good bike group or not.

For the rest of us, drafting is not normally permitted. The bike ride is therefore a time trial and you'll be riding on your own. You cannot encroach within a specified distance of the rider in front unless in the process of overtaking. And if you are overtaken by another rider, you are expected to withdraw promptly from the draft zone of the person who has just passed. That might mean having to slow down in order to drop back, which can be frustrating.

In practice, common sense has to prevail. Circumstances do not always allow for the necessary gaps to occur. But in general people adhere to the spirit of the drafting rules and a rider will be quick to let another know if they are out of order. Officials cannot be everywhere to make judgement calls.

You are riding on your own too in the sense that you cannot have outside assistance. Any punctures or mechanical problems you must sort yourself. Bystanders cannot assist or pass you food and drinks. You must carry everything you might need, although longer bike courses will have aid stations with supplies.

Normally I would take with me the three Allen keys that fit nearly all the moving parts on my bike and the wherewithal to deal with a flat tyre - spare inner tube, a couple of tyre levers and a small gas cartridge for inflation. The chances of a puncture are relatively small but it does happen and you don't know when it will. Many choose not to carry these items in a race, preferring to be minimalist. It comes down to how you feel about the risk of having to abandon the race.

I did my first triathlon in 1990 on a Dawes Warwick touring bike, the same one I used for cycling to work. As an infrequent triathlete, I continued to use this bike for many years, making modifications along the way to improve performance.

First I took off the parcel rack and mudguards. Over a 20km time trial, those changes alone made a difference of about two minutes. Then I acquired a set of narrower wheels, reducing the tyre width from 1¼ inches to 1 inch. Some clip-on tri-bars made a further difference, as did proper cycling shoes with cleats, rather than riding in running shoes with toe clips. Though difficult to quantify exactly, they all made a significant difference.

I liked my modified touring bike and found it deceptively quick despite the 27-inch wheels and six-speed rear cassette. It was 20 years old by the time I upgraded to a proper road bike in 2005 - the Trek 1500SR. I was 59 then. To begin with it didn't seem any quicker than my modified touring bike but I just had to be patient. It takes time to adjust to a new bike, especially one with different geometry and feel.

Eight years later, in 2013 when I was 67, I acquired a time trial bike, a Felt DA4. The first two rides were terrifying. It felt so different - the angle of my body, the slim profile, brake levers seemingly miles away from the position of my hands, different pressure on my neck, back and hamstrings. I needed time to feel confident I was in control.

The story of my bike enhancements is one of a very gradual progression. I wonder whether subconsciously I believed I wouldn't be doing triathlons for much longer and that it was therefore too much of an indulgence to upgrade my equipment. It was long enough before I realised it was best to keep looking forward.

Running

Those new to triathlon discover their legs feel strange when starting to run after riding a bike. The body is warmed up but the muscle groups required for running have been inactive. It is similar to the feeling experienced in a hill race when turning to run downhill after reaching the top. The legs are wobbly while different muscles are called into use. Although the sensation reduces with more familiarity, it emphasises the value of including bike-to-run sessions in your training.

Your running muscles may feel relatively fresh but after swimming and cycling, the engine powering these muscles carries some fatigue. Those with a running background may be accustomed to running when they feel tired but others will find it more of a challenge. In my early years of triathlon I could handle tired-running but my capacity for that has diminished. My engine needs to have some life in it when starting out on the run.

I run in shoes that give plenty of cushioning and protection and look for a heel-to-toe drop of 10mm minimum. For some years now I have used the Mizuno Wave Rider range and I also find Brooks very suitable. They are not particularly light and even less so with an orthotic insole, but they are what works best for me. For a quicker transition I find it helps to use shoelaces with toggles. That allows you to slip your feet into the running shoes, then all that's required is a small tug on the toggle before being off on your way.

There are fewer rules in the running section of a triathlon. There is still no external assistance permitted. You carry your own refreshments, but for longer distances or warmer temperatures there are aid stations with drinks, sponges and gels, depending on what is appropriate.

Intriguingly, the rules specify that competitors are permitted to walk but not to crawl. Can it ever get as gruelling as that? Perhaps the sight of people approaching the finish on all fours is not an image the sport wishes to portray. So remember to stay upright.

Transition

Transition is the fourth discipline - that part of the triathlon spent transferring from swimming to cycling (referred to as T1) and from cycling to running (T2).

Although they can be physically separate, normally T1 and T2 occur in the same place. It's an enclosed area where bicycles are racked along with other items of kit required for cycling and running. Each competitor will have an allotted space. At a big event the transition zone can cover an area significantly larger than two football fields.

On completing the swim, competitors run to the transition zone and proceed to where their bike is racked. You need to discard a swim cap and goggles, take off a wetsuit, put on and fasten a cycling helmet, perhaps a number belt, shades and cycling shoes unless they are already clipped to your pedals. Depending on conditions, you might need extra clothing. Then you proceed with your bike to the exit point and mount the bike after the mount line.

That is T1. It covers an assortment of tasks that too few triathletes spend sufficient time practising. Often there is much greater scope for improving your transition times by a minute than for taking 30 seconds off your swim time. Everything counts. There's no point in having a brilliant swim if you proceed to lose time unnecessarily in transition.

At the second transition, T2, you step off the bike before the dismount line and proceed on foot to return your bike to its original place beside the rest of your kit. Then it is helmet off, cycling shoes off, running shoes on and then head to the run exit.

It can be straightforward, or in the case of a large event a little more complicated. Your bike racking position will look different depending on the direction of approach and whether other competitors' bikes are alongside yours.

The effects of oxygen debt are not to be underestimated. With sweat in your eyes and your breathing ragged, the transition zone can seem like a blurred forest of bikes. I have had a catalogue of avoidable incidents in T2 that have caused delays. Losing 15 seconds needlessly means the person who was level with you at the end of the bike ride is 50m ahead when you start the run. It is a wake-up call.

So it's important to spend time beforehand working out a reliable way to recognise your position in the transition zone. Something that does not depend on objects that may move such as adjacent bikes. You need to be familiar with where the bike exit and the run exit are and above all you need to remain alert to execute the transition efficiently.

I have often struggled with wetsuit removal. You can unzip the wetsuit as soon as you come out of the water and remove the top half down to your waist while running into transition. Removal time then becomes however long it takes to get out of the bottom half once you have reached your bike. Sometimes the wetsuit comes off easily, at other times it will bunch up over my legs and take ages to peel off over ankles and feet. It's even more difficult when you have inflexible ankles and big feet. I find it requires a firm approach: two or three quick and determined pulls to get it down over the thighs, then a strong flourish to sweep it off the lower leg and clear of the feet. My latest Zone 3 wetsuit is proving to be more efficient, as the silicon cuff and ankle sections help it to slip off more easily.

I have found it instructive to watch elite competitors in transition. They are incredibly slick, like a Formula 1 pit stop. They seem able to get out of a wetsuit with a flick of the legs while simultaneously putting on and fastening their helmets. And they head through T2 - racking their bikes and putting on running shoes - while barely breaking stride.

Putting it all together

A triathlon may sound like a swim, a bike and a run. But it's a swim-bike-run and the hyphens are important.

You are not swimming as fast as you can, taking a breather in T1, then cycling as hard as you can and gathering yourself in T2 before running as quickly as possible to the finish. Increasingly I have come to understand the connections between the five elements and think in terms of 'flow', maintaining a momentum through the race.

People sometimes ask me which part I am best at. I struggle to give a straight answer, as it depends on the context. In an age group championship, my relative strengths will normally show in swimming and running because others of my age are invariably stronger cyclists. But in the general spectrum of open competition my strengths swing the other way and my bike ride is more likely to be my strongest element. Perhaps the answer is that, broadly, I'm reasonably well balanced across the disciplines.

On one occasion at a small event I came 17th out of 43 competitors. It was an open race with a random field of participants. I had the 18th best split for each of the swim, bike and run. My T1 should have been better, but it was 18th too. Perfect symmetry. There should have been a prize for that.

You want to start a triathlon with the best swim that will take the least amount of effort. Then your transition should have a well-rehearsed order, such as putting on shoes, helmet, shades, number belt, any clothing and so on, making sure everything is laid out so you can tackle it on auto-pilot.

I think of the bike and run as a continuum. I need to achieve the bike ride that will give me the best run, with T2 part of the flow. It will seldom work out as neatly as that but I find it sets the end point as the context for each component part. After the event I can look back and see what went well and what I might do differently the next time. There is always scope for improvement. This is what continually whets my appetite for the next race.

Four

RUNNING INTO TRIATHLON

For much of my working life I was in the habit of running at lunchtime. It was an easy habit to form. The first organisation I worked for had an hour and a half's break each day. Some people went home to have dinner. Others would have a three-course meal in the subsidised canteen. I went running.

In Edinburgh, with Holyrood Park close by, I had time to have a meaningful run, often meeting up with others and having a bite to eat afterwards.

Our office hours were not unusual: dinner was what you had in the middle of the day. But patterns did change. Dinners became lunches and lunches became sandwich breaks. 90 minutes for dinner in the 1960s became the lunch hour of the 1970s, which by the 1990s had become a lunch break with offices remaining open for business while staff staggered their downtime.

I moved on too, working in even better surroundings with a sports complex on site. The running habit remained. I would go for a swim in the pool if I was injured or if I was squeezed for time, on the basis that I could easily tire myself out swimming for 20 minutes. When we moved house I started cycling to and from work, a distance of about three miles. In hindsight my trajectory towards triathlon had already begun.

Then Jim, a work colleague, suggested I come along to the Saturday morning swim session with the triathlon club.

Up until that point I had been swimming without giving any thought to technique. Coming from a running background and knowing my centre of gravity was in the wrong place I accepted that I would be a weak swimmer. Swimming was a form of exercise and as long as it tired me out easily it was serving a useful purpose.

Although the swim session at the triathlon club was organised, there was only one coach and the coaching impact at individual level was necessarily limited. I went along for the exercise and the training environment without thinking of doing a triathlon. And an hour of swimming really did tire me out.

I took part eventually in my first triathlon and I enjoyed it, using my commuting bike minus mudguards and parcel rack. My main recollection is of how long I took in transition to pull on a long-sleeved tightly-fitting Helly Hansen over a wet body - I struggled for ages and it seemed to take longer than the time I'd spent swimming.

Although a regular at the weekly swim session, I didn't do another triathlon for a further three years. With my first event in 1990 and my second in 1993, my association with triathlon was very gradual. Of course, there were far fewer events at that time. It probably wasn't until the end of the 1990s before the number of events and participants grew significantly.

I competed sparingly over the following years - a combination of work commitments and increasing difficulty keeping clear of injury when running. But I continued to attend the swim sessions regularly and cycling was fine, but apart from orienteering, which was helpful because it was mostly off-road, I rarely ran.

Even with orienteering, I was frequently derailed by leg problems. Many of these, particularly issues with my Achilles tendon, went back a long time - to the days before proper running shoes were commonly available. Eventually Chris, my wife, persuaded me to see a physiotherapist and get myself sorted.

The physiotherapist's name was Jane. She diagnosed immediately that I had a foot problem requiring orthotic support. Without this support, particularly when running, an abnormal strain was being placed on the Achilles and calves, causing repeated breakdowns. She referred me on to a podiatrist called Alison, who carried out an assessment and arranged for bespoke orthotic insoles to correct the misalignments. When these were in place I returned to Jane, who got to work on the damaged tissue. Within a few weeks she had me running again.

It was not all plain sailing. There were frequent regress-ions of one kind or another. But Jane worked miracles to keep me going. She wasn't fazed by the setbacks, always finding solutions and with her encouragement I was able to think of returning to proper competitions.

Later that year, 2005, I took part in a sprint triathlon and went on to do further races. It was a real transformation. Though lacking running fitness, I was running and I was enjoying it. However, I was cautious to avoid hard surfaces as much as possible and was frequently relying on Jane's extraordinary ability to keep me on the rails.

The 2006 season was planned to put me in the right place for the following year, when I would be retiring from work and have the time and opportunity to focus more on my sport and go to events further afield.

Having already become the Scottish 'Vintage' Champion (for aged 60+) at Lochore Meadows on my 60th birthday, I finished my season at the Standard Distance Champion-ships at Strathclyde Park in September. My intention was to do enough to qualify for the European Age Group Championships in Copenhagen the following year. Finish-ing second in my age group, I succeeded. Everything was ready for when I would retire the following year.

Although I did a number of triathlons in 2006, my training was erratic due to continual niggling problems of one kind or another. I could do little training of substance between races but the races themselves became a form of rehabilitation, clearing away several issues. Physio Jane did some remarkable work over that period to keep me going and was a great source of encouragement.

And so, shortly after retiring in 2007, I was able to take part in my first international age group championship.

It was the European Championships in Copenhagen and I was in the 60-64 category. There was only one race, held over the Standard distance (1,500m swim, 40km cycle and 10km run). I was one of three competitors from Britain in my age group and finished 5th out of the 11 who took part - a very low number of competitors compared to the years that followed (see Appendix 1, for more detail).

It was a completely new experience, living in the pretence that I was a full-time athlete for two or three days, fully focused on preparing for my race.

It was also my first experience of travelling with a bike. Fortunately I set about packing my bike several days before departure, as it took most of that time to get all the bits into the box and close the lid. I had never before dismantled the bike for this purpose and it didn't cooperate particularly well.

The first problem was removing the pedals. I couldn't shift them. The local bike shop guys gave me a few tips on how to loosen the pedals and sold me a large spanner that would do the job properly. I was on a steep learning curve. Though much more competent now, packing the bike box is still a task I don't try to do in a hurry.

There was a British contingent of about 250 men and women spread across a range of five-year age groups from 20 to 70 - none of whom I knew. I was billeted with Mark who was in a much younger age group than mine. He knew a few of the others and kindly included me with his friends when they went for a meal or a foray into town. It was a supportive atmosphere.

I enjoyed the thrill of the big-race experience: cycling and running on closed city-centre roads, crowds of spectators, the finish line in the city's main square. We swam in the sea alongside ships at the waterfront on Christians Brygge. The water was quite cold - literally Baltic - and some of the older competitors decided not to start. But it wasn't a problem for me after what I had been experiencing at home.

Some of the younger women's age groups started in a wave a few minutes after mine and I remember the leaders came swarming over us as we approached the swim exit. The older competitors - older than my 60-64 age group - had chairs provided beside their bikes in transition, but unfortunately this practice appears to have lapsed.

There was a long linear transition zone and then four 10km laps on the bike on a fairly flat course with several sharp corners and some tight roundabouts. And there was quite a stiff wind to contend with.

The run course was a single lap with multiple changes of direction that made it difficult to judge how far there was still to go. But eventually I caught sight of the blue carpet -

the distinctive branding associated with ETU and ITU events for the final approach and then we were in the main square crossing the finishing line in front of the town hall.

Though I was only too aware that it was not a represent-ative result - there were many back home who would have finished ahead of me - it was a spectacular experience and I enjoyed every minute of it.

But it was watching the elite competitors racing the following day to become European Champions that left the greatest impression.

I had never seen this level of racing up close. I was totally in awe of the speed and intensity of it, the uninterrupted flow through all the component elements. It gave me a new perspective on what triathlon racing is about and a sense that I was somehow a part of it. I too was a participant in the championships, racing on the same course the day before against my contemporaries. An exhilarating feeling, one I realised I'd like to experience again.

The next opportunity followed in the autumn of that same year. Several of us from Stirling Triathlon Club had qualified to take part in the World Age Group Champion-ships in Hamburg. We learnt that a Sprint distance event was being introduced to the Championships for the first time, to run alongside the Standard distance. This was wel-come news to me, as I preferred the sprint distances.

I teamed up with club-mate Andy who had been quick off the mark in making travel and accommodation arrangements. We flew to Hamburg via Frankfurt where more people boarded the plane. Some were clearly going to the triathlon event too, one of whom took the empty seat beside mine. After a while we started talking. His name was Jan. I told him that I was taking part in the 60-64 sprint distance race and asked him what category he was in, to which he responded with commendable good humour that he was in the elite race.

Andy, listening to this on my other side, was entertained by my naivety. Jan went on to say that he was hoping to gain selection for the German team at the following year's Olympic games in Beijing but would need to finish in the first six in the elite race and be one of the first three Germans. We had a good conversation and he was generous in asking about my own aspirations. Leaving the plane at Hamburg, we wished each other well and I said I would look out for Jan in his race and give him a shout.

This was a bigger occasion than Copenhagen, with more participants and road closures for the whole course. The transition area was more than half a kilometre long, running the length of a street and once all the bikes were racked the scene resembled the railway station in Amsterdam. I worked out that when entering the transition zone I would have to go 350m along the line of bikes before reaching mine.

We swam in Alster Lake in the centre of Hamburg. The water was opaque and towards the end we swam underneath a long and very low bridge. It was like going through a dark tunnel, knuckles almost grazing the underside of the bridge with each stroke.

We exited the water at the side of the Radhaus Platz. Event marshals pulled us out of the water onto a ramp - but perhaps they were just pulling out the people who looked as though they needed help.

From there I ran some 500m barefoot over uneven cobbles covered by a thin carpet to reach the transition zone, at which point the 350m stretch to my bike began. That was followed by a further 200m run in bike shoes before reaching the mount line. All in all, the transition from swim to bike involved running more than a kilometre without proper running shoes, something well out of my comfort zone.

The 20km bike course itself was two undulating laps on closed roads. At the time I felt I'd had a good bike ride but later the results would show that my time relative to others in my age category was not as good as I thought.

In amongst a crowd of competitors, your direct opponents are those in the same age group who started in the same swim wave. All competitors were 'body marked' on the back of the lower leg with a marker pen to indicate the age category and that meant it was possible to tell whether the person in front was an opponent or not. So although more people passed me on the run course than I overtook, I knew I had gained a few places before the finish.

Just like in Copenhagen, the finish line was right in the city centre at the Radhaus Platz. Fifth place once again too, less than a couple of minutes away from a podium position. Meanwhile club-mate Andy finished fourth in his age group, losing out to third place by just five seconds - a great result, so close to a medal.

Reflecting on my race afterwards I realised that I lacked a plan, particularly at the start of the swim. I was in a swim wave of around 150 competitors consisting of the older male age groups - all those aged 50 and over. I should have been more alert and tried to keep better contact with the main bunch but I was relatively inexperienced. I've found I have a tendency to swim at the same pace as those around me and on this occasion I had allowed myself to settle in with the wrong group.

The distance covered in transition from swim to bike was also a problem as I lost time having to run carefully in bare feet over a difficult surface without proper orthotic support. There was a great deal to take on board from the bike ride and the run too. It was a huge learning experience in a big race atmosphere - something I could not have found at home and was exhilarated to be part of.

Spectators lined the streets several deep for the elite races the following day. Theirs was a different course - more compact and spectator-friendly with multiple laps for the bike and run routes. They were good races to watch and I looked out for my new pal Jan to give him encouragement. He did well, finishing sixth and the second German, so he would make the team for the Beijing Olympics. A cause for celebration.

Fast-forward 11 months to the following summer and

as you'll remember I got up in the middle of the night to watch the men's triathlon at the Beijing Olympics and found with astonishment that, not long before, I had been rubbing shoulders with the new Olympic champion. Forgetting that the person I sat next to on the plane to Hamburg would be in the race, it came as a bolt from the blue.

Jan Frodeno was an unexpected winner of the gold medal. He was not the top-ranked German at the time. That was Daniel Unger who finished in sixth place. But Frodeno was at the start of a career that would see him at or near the top of the sport for many years.

Four years later, when I volunteered at the London Olympics, I watched Jan finish 5th and was able to give a shout of encouragement there too amongst the noise of a huge crowd. Because I was part of the 'field of play' team positioned on the path round the Serpentine, the runners went past me four times just inches away.

After London Frodeno turned his attention more to longer distances, 70.3 and full Ironman, winning the Ironman World Championship at Hawaii in 2015 and 2016 before setting a record time in 2019.

The people you come across through your sport.

Five
PHYSICAL FUNCTIONALITY

I climb out of the water onto the bottom rung of a long flight of metal-grille steps leading to the quayside above. It's unbearable in bare feet but at last the blue carpeting at the top comes into sight as welcome relief. Thin and loose, the carpet is not comfortable for long. It has shifted and wrinkled with the footfall, masking unevenness in the paving beneath and, worse still, the unseen rail tracks.

It's my 71st birthday - events have a habit of coinciding with my birthdays - and I'm in the docklands of Düsseldorf.

The transition zone resembles a fortress. Enclosed within security fencing along the length of a narrow street, it runs parallel to and a block away from the waterfront. There are things to do as I head in its direction, principally getting hold of the zipper cord dangling from the back of my neck and pulling it down so that I can peel the wetsuit off my shoulders and pull my arms out of the sleeves. Soon I have the wetsuit down to my waist, ready to slip out of the bottom half as soon as I reach my bike.

When we racked our bikes the previous afternoon I took careful note of its position. My spot is at least 200m along the line of closely racked bikes. Fortunately there is a distinctive doorway that creates a good marker point.

The layout of the transition area is very tidy and we are expected to keep it that way, putting all discarded kit - goggles, swim cap, wetsuit and anything else - into the small plastic crate each competitor has been allocated. Anything left outside the crate, even hanging over the lip, is liable to incur a penalty of some kind.

I arrive at my bike and start pulling the wetsuit down over my hips, legs and feet. This is where balance and agility are required. My aim is to accomplish the manoeuvre standing up but I'm breathing too hard and my pulse isn't calm enough.

I peel the wetsuit down to my knees but when it comes to the lower legs I can't keep my balance any longer and have to sit down on the ground. Not the most efficient way to get out of a wetsuit but the only one in the circumstances - and there's still a measure of agility required. The final bit is a struggle, pulling the folds of the wetsuit clear of large feet and inflexible ankles.

I need to find a better way of doing this. I'm reminded that when I first took part in a European age group championship 10 years previously, chairs were provided in the transition area for those of more advanced years. That would have done nicely but we're all equal now. No one receives special treatment.

Actually my balance is better than it used to be. Some years ago I couldn't stand on one leg for as long as others could with their eyes closed. However, through doing regular exercises my balance has improved significantly.

Nowadays I spend a lot more time on exercises for mobility and functionality than I ever did before. Without the ability to perform the actions and range of movements your sport entails, you cannot enjoy practising it. So my priority is to look after my physical functionality.

I am supported in this by Anne, the performance physiotherapist I see on a regular basis for review and maintenance. She specialises in injury prevention and is also a movement and fitness coach. If she had a mission statement it would be helping people to get the best out of themselves.

Working with Anne, I have developed disciplined routines using a roller for massaging leg and gluteal muscles and performing a range of exercises for mobility and core stability. Some, referred to as 'teeth cleaning', are carried out daily, others twice or three times a week. I find it works best to do the routines before breakfast. Then it becomes a habit that doesn't encroach on the rest of the day. The exercises are reviewed regularly. It seems that as soon as I become proficient at any, I am moved on to a more challenging exercise.

Starting from a low base it took time to make a difference but huge strides have been made. It feels as though I spent most of my later 60s working towards a level of functionality I wish I'd had 20 years before.

The exercises tackle the attributes required for swimming, cycling and running - core stability, trunk rotation and counter-rotation, balance and agility issues. And Anne also takes a close interest in whether I am accomplishing my transitions as effectively as I should.

So I have foam and grid rollers, a mini trampoline (or trampet) and a gym ball as basic equipment as well as an accumulation of small rubber balls and stretch bands. The watchwords are 'symmetry' and 'effortless control'. Any exercise done on one side of the body should be replicated on the other side. It has certainly made a significant difference and it has been an enjoyable process.

For a long time I was resistant to going to the gym, being much happier doing exercises that were possible to do at home. But I have come to appreciate that the gym has an important place in a balanced exercise programme. It is a training session in its own right, not a marginal activity slipped in before or after a run or a swim. This attitude makes gym sessions more worthwhile. And I am convinced of the benefits they give to your overall performance. Being strong from the inside out enhances and maintains your performance when your body is tiring.

The volume and particularly the intensity of training sessions has reduced over the years but the sessions have become more purposeful, set in the context of a bigger plan: to enjoy being able to do my sport and, within the context of my circumstances, to try and do it well.

I have applied much more focus to technique, moving efficiently and distributing effort more evenly. As the capacity to recover from exertion in-race becomes more difficult than it was in the past - for example getting back into your stride after being in oxygen debt for a period - an even distribution of effort becomes much more important. So I think about how I can do the quickest swim that will take the least out of myself, or cycling in the optimal way to set me up for the run to follow.

It is easy to let your horizon become narrower, to retreat to your comfort zone, which makes it essential to broaden out by doing things differently. For me the programmes of exercises are my gateway to training and participating in races. I'm training less intensely these days, with greater attention given to efficiency of movement and technique - all part of a regime of training smarter not harder.

When running, it's disconcerting that you can feel good and believe you have been going well only to be disillusioned by the stopwatch. Other things being equal, it has to be accepted that when comparing yourself against what you may have done in the past, it is inevitable: you are likely to be slower.

You may be running with the same rhythm and the same effort, but if there is less power in the drive, not quite as much spring in the step, your stride will be slightly shorter.

It took some time to learn that comparison with the past can only lead to disappointment. The focus should be on the present, in the context of the circumstances in which your performance took place - personal ones such as state of preparedness, fitness and health, as well as other external factors. Satisfaction instead comes from how close you come to feeling you have done the best possible.

With ageing there is less elasticity in the muscles. I have come to learn the importance of making sure that all the muscle groups in the chain, particularly the posterior chain, are awake and functioning when I exercise. Any muscle not contributing its proper functionality merely places greater stress in other areas. This explains why loosening the muscles of the lower back, for example, may be the treatment required for tightness in the hamstrings or calf muscles.

The same principle of interconnectedness from head to foot applies to the anterior chain and the diagonal ones. Looking after yourself is important as injuries can take a long time to clear and may leave a legacy of weakness. I've found that soft tissue injuries are most likely to occur when engaged in some unaccustomed activity, particularly when unprepared. In other words, don't run for a bus without first doing a proper warm up.

Older athletes are seldom free from injury. Indeed it can feel disconcerting to be injury free. A few niggling issues provide a comfort zone. It's a proportional relationship. It's about how you manage these things; to accept them and work with them, not fight against them, by adapting and modifying. Warming up thoroughly becomes increasingly important, as does giving proper attention to warming down. Keep in control of what you are doing; in a group activity be wary of inappropriate volume or intensity that may only be suiting others. You don't have to prove anything. It's about fun and enjoyment - switched on fun, not switched off.

Anyway. Back to the race in Düsseldorf, where at last I have the wetsuit clear of my feet and I make sure everything is deposited properly in my numbered crate.

With helmet, shades and cycling shoes on, I run with the bike to the transition exit. My left hand is on the saddle but otherwise I'm running normally - as normally as running in cycling shoes permits.

I am able to steer my way through the corridor of bikes and competitors without really thinking about it. It's a skill acquired 60 years ago when cycling to school, which I did almost every day for a number of years. We had to dismount at the school gate and walk with our bikes to the bike sheds and there was the same routine at the end of the day. I became well practised at manoeuvring the bike with one hand on the saddle, most likely engaged in conversation, while weaving a path through groups of jostling people. I learned more things at school than I realise.

My pedal cranks are parallel to the ground, held in position by two rubber bands stretched between the left pedal and the quick-release lever on the rear wheel. Bands from the tops of jars of homemade marmalade do the job neatly;

looped together they can just stretch the distance without breaking. It means the right-hand pedal is at three o'clock ready for the shoe to slip in when I come to mount the bike.

That's the theory. While the crank might be correctly aligned, the pedal itself may require a little footwork to find connection with the cleat but I find the arrangement sufficiently effective. As only one of the bands will burst with the first pedal stroke, the pieces of rubber remain attached and don't cause litter.

I've gone quite a distance before finally reaching the mount line, slipping my feet into the pedals and setting out on the bike course. From finishing the swim to mounting the bike I must have covered at least 800m and I find out afterwards it took nearly five minutes. It's a significant element of the race in a big championship event, one that provides considerable scope for being smarter.

You learn a great deal by watching others. As a volunteer marshal at the British Triathlon Super Series event at Strathclyde Park, stationed at the transition exit, I had a good view of competitors mounting their bikes. Some were expert; they ran out of transition in bare feet, bike shoes already in the pedals, and in a single flowing movement without breaking stride hopped onto the saddle and were away. It looked so easy.

Of the others, many came out of transition wearing cycling shoes and then mounted their bikes, some very efficiently and others much less so. But what struck me was the number who had really complicated arrangements - bike shoes fixed to the pedals and arrays of rubber bands to hold things in place - and then took a long time mounting their bikes and trying to get their feet into their bike shoes, wobbling while attempting to fasten them, blocking other riders and sometimes stopping to begin all over again.

The message was clear: simplicity is the ultimate sophistication. Only fix your bike shoes to the pedals if you can do the whole thing efficiently, mounting the bike cleanly and fastening up the shoes after riding off. Otherwise, a lot of time is saved by putting the bike shoes on in transition and efficiently mounting your bike. It informed my present strategy, one I find effective while also keeping within the limits of my agility.

With most things I've found it more worthwhile to concentrate on not losing time unnecessarily, rather than trying to save seconds by doing something that can lose much more if not done properly. I much prefer the concept of 'flow' through a race. Of using well-tested routines all building towards the final outcome and avoiding expenditure of the emotional energy that occurs when urgency and intensity intervene. It's much better to set out on the bike course feeling calm with everything having gone as planned rather than in a state of agitation.

That year I did 9 triathlons and 2 aquathlons but had still not settled into a consistent pattern with my race nutrition. When I came to review my 2017 season, it was noticeable that my better performances had occurred when I hadn't consumed any gels or energy bars. So I decided to stick to taking nothing in-race for Sprint distances the following year, starting with Abu Dhabi.

I made some other observations too. The wetsuit removal problems had been solved during the course of the year. As much as anything it came down to an attitude of mind, being firm and positive. Also there were adjustments I could make that would benefit my running. Physio Anne's input, combined with advice from coach Bob, helped to identify what I could work on. These were issues I could look at over the winter.

Six

MENTAL STRENGTH COACHING

It's late February. I'm in Abu Dhabi having a video call with Kim in Bristol. We're debriefing following my warm-up race in the sprint triathlon at TriYas, discussing what I will take forward from it to enhance my performance in the Abu Dhabi Triathlon two weeks later.

A hot dry wind made conditions at TriYas oppressive. I had cycled quite strongly but the stretches against the stiff wind had been challenging, like riding into a hairdryer, sucking all the moisture out of me.

I tell Kim how I took too much out of myself on the bike - and was not carrying enough water - and as a consequence I was in real difficulty when it came to the run. At times I'd been reduced to a walk, but at least there were others suffering similarly. I report that I've got hold of a bottle cage to attach behind the saddle next time for additional water supplies. But the main thing we talk about is the need to be more careful. In such conditions I need to keep well within myself on the bike ride.

Kim suggests I should be aware of whether I have a limiting mindset on the bike ride as this can distract focus, cause frustration and be energy draining. Yet she acknowledges that it is normal in any situation for those wanting to achieve their best.

The key is to be myself. What can I do, think and feel to be more helpful and in turn positive with my focus. Can I convert "keeping well within myself" into something positive?

Our conversation explores this and fortunately I am speaking to a skilled practitioner. In response to her probing I admit that I need to be riding to a level that will allow me to have a good running performance. And eventually I take it a step further:

"I'll focus on having the best bike ride to give me the best run."

I've got there. There's been quite a lot of steering required but I've got there. I've worked out the strategy for myself and they are my words. I have ownership of it.

We touch on some other things and discuss thoughts on a model of excellence (MoE) for the race - identifying people who epitomise attributes and skills that I would like to make use of. I say that it should be someone who performs with a cool attitude in difficult conditions. I'm going to consider this a bit more but I mention a couple of names I have in mind.

Finally, we talk about how I have become the subject of some media interest. This happened after I was identified as the oldest person in the race. Though enjoyable, it has added pressure of an unfamiliar kind. Any pressure I feel needs to enhance my internal focus. I take up Kim's suggestion of making a mind map to figure out how I want to manage this interest while still being my best.

In my early 60s I had a major surgical repair to my Achilles tendon. Problems with my Achilles went back many years, affecting my ability to run, but it finally broke down completely.

My choice was to abandon thoughts of continuing to run and cycle, or undergo surgery. I decided to follow the surgical route and suffice to say it was a major repair. I was sidelined for a season, which later developed into the better part of a second season. I did return eventually but with a legacy of inhibitions.

Rehabilitation became as much a mental issue as a physical one. I needed to overcome concerns - fear even - that everything might break down again.

This led me to work with Kim, one of the therapists with the GB age group team, who thought she could help me using mental strength coaching techniques. But it would take time and commitment. She certainly appeared to recognise and understand the nature of my problem in a way that others I had spoken to had not. From the outset we established the coaching relationship as a partnership.

Kim introduced me to a completely fresh landscape. She asked me to send over my race schedule for the following season. I didn't have one. Feeling unable to plan very far ahead, I'd never had one that was written down. At most it was a rough idea. The request came as a signal that I was being regarded as a serious athlete and immediately my horizon was lifted beyond the next race. I set to and drew up what looked like a realistic plan and sent it over.

Then it was suggested I indicate objectives for each of the events, listing any limiting factors - physical or circumstantial - that could affect whether these objectives might be achieved and say what I would need to do in order to counter them. It made me stop and think. I realised that I could think of all kinds of limiting factors. Some of these I could counter but others were less straightforward. Within a short space of time, not only had my thoughts shifted beyond the next race but the horizon of my aspirations was opening out.

Training sessions were given a purpose. They could focus on a particular aspect of the race or on how I was going to feel while doing it. It could be my body position on the bike or my breathing when running, my leg cadence when running or cycling. Alternatively my goal might simply be to relax and enjoy the session. There was flexibility if circumstances required a change but there would always be a purpose or intent, no vacuum.

I learned to work with the factors that might affect my ability to perform, not fight against them; to be comfortable about getting uncomfortable. My perceived limits were challenged - don't and not were banished from my vocabulary. Instead I was developing a growth mindset: what will I need to do, how will I do it, what changes do I need to make? It was about taking ownership of a situation and working out how to do the best possible given the circumstances.

Rather than advise me what I should do in any particular situation, Kim talked things over with me and posed questions that I should ask myself. The answers could result in further questions, honing the way I made decisions.

But crucially the decisions were mine and I understood how they had been reached. The process gave me ownership and accountability. I was being pushed out of my comfort zone and being made accountable but it also made things happen and increased my enjoyment of training and racing.

After each of our discussions there are action points, which involve a commitment to do some writing. It's like training for the brain, as writing down your thoughts will uncover whether sense can be made of them and that provides the clarity to take plans forward. Writing it all down while everything is fresh in the mind is important, as memory moves on. Discipline is required to ensure the learnings are taken on board and acted upon.

It was about learning, always learning; training smarter not harder. Locking in the learnings, converting them into gains.

Initially I regarded Kim as a facilitator, helping me to overcome a mental blockage arising from a specific issue. After a while I realised that she was a mind coach for performance. Yet it was more than that. Quite simply she was my performance coach. The focus was on planning, preparation and performance.

The barriers I encountered along the way started to slip aside to clear a pathway. Limitations could of course be authentic but those which were supposed or imagined were marginalised. I could create an environment for having the best race possible.

I was in a privileged position to have such a coach, one whose support helped me achieve a level of performance beyond what I believed was possible. But as well as being a GB age group athlete in her own right, Kim is a triathlon coach, so this development should not have come as a surprise.

Over time the concerns that led me to seek help in the first place became marginalised. I was focusing on a bigger picture and I was enjoying my sport. It was mental strength training, a concept I had not come across before. And it was proving effective.

Mental strength training has several facets. There is the practical, pragmatic, common sense element - planning and organisation, creating a structure for how you do things so that they happen in an effective way, clearing away the things that don't need to be there. It's about observing how others do things and learning from them where you can. And learning from yourself as well.

The more complex area of mental strength training is the emotional side, the part that has shades of colour - feelings, attitudes, mindset. Confidence, belief in yourself and what is possible, focus, sense of purpose, being 'present', ability to deal with the unexpected, awareness of what you can control and what you can't. The list is extensive. As individuals we possess these attributes to a greater or lesser extent and they will vary according to context. We must look to build these attributes and develop them so we can harness them in the right context.

For triathlons, ideally the combination of physical effort and mental application should blend to give the optimum outcome.

Each autumn the next season is planned. Having a race schedule seems very basic but it is important as it establishes the context for your planning. You need to plan your season, put it down in writing, including the events you would like to do and that will fit in with family plans or other commitments.

Then consider which event or events will be your main ones and assign levels of priority. Consider as well the relationship between events and the space between them. Less important races can be used as preparation for the more important ones.

Normally I would have three levels of priority, labelling them A, B and C. I would then limit the A priority to two, or at most three, events. Mini-peaks around which to organise the season.

I have also come to appreciate that when a series of events is used as preparation for a high-priority race, you can accumulate psychological momentum. So long as you focus on how each event can enhance preparation for the main goal.

I started testing this concept for the 2017 and 2018 seasons. Finding that it added purpose to the race plan and was proving remarkably effective, I implemented it fully in 2019.

The 2019 season fitted conveniently into three distinct phases - priority A events in early March, mid July and the beginning of September. For each of these events I was able to schedule two additional events during the prior month as a lead-in. That gave three blocks of three events with a goal at the end of each block. And as things worked out it was successful. I could feel my performance progression with each passing block.

At an early stage a discipline developed. After each race, before the end of that day - so it is still fresh in the memory - I write down the things that have gone well. I list three things at most. I also write down not more than two things that could have been better, adding a note about what I would do differently next time.

Note that the list is kept short, always containing more things that went well than could have been better. It is the writing that is important; thoughts and memories are not sufficient.

And it's significant that it is you yourself who is identifying what might be done differently another time. It puts ownership and control into your own hands and sharing the information adds accountability. You become aware of what aspects have to be locked in and kept secure as well as the things that require work.

Ideally the process should evolve so that those featuring amongst the things that could have been better should eventually start to appear alongside those that went well.

Gradually I've been introduced to various techniques. They comprise a collection of tools, to be used on their own or in combination according to circumstances. Some are techniques you might hear elite performers referring to and that gives added frisson.

Visualisation was one of the earlier techniques I adopted - the mental rehearsal of imagining yourself going through a race and embedding the image in your mind. It helps you to feel familiar with the race when it starts, to be 'present' and fully engaged with it.

Visualise yourself doing an event - from how you feel at the start to what you will do during each part of the race through to the finish. An effective time to do this is the evening before. Just sit in a chair, close your eyes and take yourself through it.

Visualisation can be applied to the whole race or alternatively to parts of it that require a particular focus. In addition, it can be useful to visualise yourself through the eyes of an onlooker - what you would look like to someone who is watching you. It helps to settle in your mind the full perspective of the race and can help you pick up on things you might want to question or change.

In my first season of experimenting with visualisation I was usually picking up issues to do with T1. This led me to discard socks for racing, which made a significant difference to transition times without any downside. It also made me question why I was putting my number belt on in transition when I could already have it on under my wetsuit. So I made this change and discovered that many others already did the same. Only non-wetsuit swims require you to put on and fasten the belt in transition. This change saved a little time, which all makes a difference - psychologically at the very least.

One issue cropping up frequently was a tendency to lose concentration towards the end of the bike ride. I would slow down without realising it. Kim asked what I would do that could make a difference. Endeavouring to be vigilant and take extra care not to lose concentration lacked a positive action.

Further probing guided me round to a positive action point, which was to say: "If I lose concentration I will do a, b and c". And I had to work out what a, b and c were. I came up with the action points that I believed would work: get onto the tri-bars, hold cadence of 85 minimum and keep an eye on the speed.

Incidentally, I have not had cause to implement the action plan. The new regime had the effect of keeping me fully focused the whole time. Losing concentration - at least in that context - has not been a problem.

I realised the benefit of always having a plan, even if it is a low-key race or the objective is to have fun. If you have 'switched on' fun it will be much more rewarding than 'switched off' fun. I have been encouraged to write things down, as it can sometimes only be when writing that you discover a thought actually exists.

Each race should have its own plan, a plan that is relevant and contemporary, not a regurgitated one. In that way you get 'present' with a race, properly engaged with it, and the whole experience is then much more satisfying. Race preparation is a personal thing. There is no right or wrong way; it is about doing what works for you. An objective and a plan, properly set out, is the framework on which to build your race and get the most from it.

Observe others racing. Look for things that could enhance your own performance. Weigh the risk of changing something against the possibility that it could make a big difference. Each autumn Kim will ask what I am going to do differently over the coming winter. It's a good discipline to refresh your approach and consider introducing different habits. It provides a reminder to reflect on what is working and the stimulus to consider ways of being smarter.

A helpful tool I mentioned earlier is the use of models of excellence (MoE), identifying people with particular qualities you would like to have more of. They could be well-known people, though often it is more effective when it's someone you know. You could have a MoE for running or for transitions, or MoEs for specific situations such as composure before a race or performing at your best on the day. You can then imagine yourself in these situations as that person.

Observe what they do - ask them about it if there is the opportunity - and think of any changes you could make to what you do. Your collection of MoEs should be continually reviewed. Keep refreshing them, introducing new ones for particular situations when a specific attribute is important.

I was introduced to the concept of being 'in the moment', achieving that state of calmness where you let go of all thoughts and allow yourself to just 'be' - your awareness and focus present and relaxed.

After you get past the point of resistance, your movements should be effortless. You're working really hard but the body is working with you to make it happen. Having experimented, I have found it possible to achieve this state when cycling - a sensation of working effortlessly hard. Similarly too in swimming I have found that opportunities to be 'in the moment' can arise.

Top athletes can be 'in the moment' throughout a race but to an even further level. Having achieved this state, they expand their vision outwards to have an awareness of what is around them. A kind of peripheral 'in the moment' vision. I reckon to have experienced this once, at the world aqua-thlon championships in Denmark when various external factors created an unusually heightened state of awareness. And I maintained it throughout the whole race. Such experiences all add to the fascination of racing.

I've never had a coach before but now I have two - one for the operating system and one for the software. It's often said that performance in sport is 70% mental and 30% physical. I wouldn't dissent from that. The three of us work as a team. I look after my sport-specific training, physio Anne develops the platform of physical functionality to help me get the best out of myself and Kim is the cohesive element for delivering the component of the mind. There's real synergy and it's highly productive. That's why I recommend creating your own team. You'll experience added enjoyment, support and enhanced performance.

Two weeks after my video call with Kim, the Abu Dhabi Triathlon begins.

We start on the beach at the water's edge, my wave consisting of all the men aged 45+. There isn't the oppressive heat I encountered at TriYas but it's hot nonetheless and care will be required.

In a combative sense the race is rough to begin with but I am able to break clear of the melee. Following some effective coaching at the club over the winter this aspect of my game is now better than it has ever been and I am well up in the group coming out of the water.

When cycling, I focus on being 'in the moment', doing the best bike ride to give me the best run. It isn't the quickest ride possible but it is controlled and absolutely fit for purpose.

When you're running, it's difficult trying to drink from a cup. There's a lot of uncomfortable gulping and very little of the contents may end up inside you. With that in mind I walk through the aid stations to rehydrate properly, dousing my head and shoulders, and run comfortably the rest of the way without wilting.

Someone wearing headphones grabs me as I cross the finish line. A camera and a big furry rabbit home in close and an interview begins. Somehow I am composed enough to participate and it's possible I may have said some coherent things. I gathered it was material for a highlights programme. Later it emerged that I hadn't only won the 'M65+' category, I was also ahead of the first finisher in M60-64. In that context, when local journalists call me to ask how the race has gone, I don't mind the attention.

Of all my races so far, this was the one where I'd done

very much my own thing, controlling my own pace, ignoring others. And that meant after the cycle I felt ready to run at optimum. For the first time I was conscious of having made a shift from racing to performing.

Seven

IN THE WATER

I'm in the sea off Denmark. It's summer and the hottest part of a very hot day. Lined up for an aquathlon, treading water, we're waiting for the start hooter to sound.

I'm highly alert but oddly there's no sign of jellyfish. At the swim-course familiarisation the day before, the water was teeming with the creatures - clusters of pale translucent discs everywhere. Nearly all who went in the water were stung.

I know what a jellyfish sting is like. It feels sharper than a nettle sting and can leave a rash that remains irritable for a few days. I preferred to avoid acquiring that discomfort before the race but was prepared to put up with it on the day. Fortunately we were going to be permitted to wear wetsuits. We were also advised to smear Vaseline on faces, hands and feet.

The start hooter sounds. I try to start quickly so I can tuck in behind another swimmer who might pull me along in his slipstream.

Today it seems the jellyfish have moved on. But the potential to encounter them has put me in a state of heightened awareness. My swim feels different from any previously. For the first time I experience that sensation of peripheral vision I mentioned in the previous chapter, while being completely focused 'in the moment'.

I swim alongside other competitors' feet rather than directly behind them. That way I keep contact with others and benefit from slipstreaming but also have a much clearer view. I am looking up and ahead for navigation, down and ahead for jellyfish and can keep an eye on what is happening around me. It becomes easy to spot opportunities to move forward and latch onto other swimmers.

Then, turning into the more sheltered water of the marina, the jellyfish begin to appear.

In the shafts of sunlight the shoals look rather beautiful, sparkling like illuminated chandeliers. I encourage myself by assuming the swimmers ahead might have cleared a channel for those of us following but it doesn't seem too evident. While hoping for the best, the occasional wee nip is a reminder that they are not fairy lights and provide the necessary incentive to keep pressing on.

Reaching the transition zone I look along the line of baskets for my age category but only my German friend

Herbert has a wetsuit in his. All the other baskets are empty, running shoes beside them. Herbert said the day before that the two of us would have to do well. I haven't let him down so far.

I follow through with one of my best transitions. Perhaps I need to be chased more often by a metaphorical pitchfork. I am certainly switched on. Performance is converging with opportunity.

Swimming is the least natural of the triathlon disciplines. I say that because you have to learn to swim - and you probably need lessons. You don't need to learn how to run. You do need to learn to ride a bike, but most people do that while they're youngsters. And, as they say, once you learn to ride a bike, it's not something you forget.

Swimming once a week is fine. But if you wish to improve you need to be in the water twice a week, preferably three times. It's a discipline that can get rusty - through lack of contact with water. If you miss a few weeks it may take a while to get back to where you were. So to keep on top, triathletes have to be regular swimmers.

My swimming has gradually improved. That's encouraging considering other things are slowing down.

After retiring in 2007 I took a triathlon coaching qualification - the club was looking for more coaches, especially to run the swim sessions. Being a coach makes me think more about how I do things myself. It has also made me more receptive to input from other coaches.

Improvement came throughout my 60s, with a major breakthrough at the age of 68 through the input of coaches Shaun and Bob. In the end it was small things to do with technique - when pointed out, explained well and taken on board - that made a difference.

From that point I gained the confidence to try aquathlon events. And more recently towards the end of 2019 I've had further input from Alan, of Scottish Swimming, who has helped me to achieve more with less effort. Swimming used to be the weakest of my triathlon disciplines but now, in some contexts, it has become my strongest.

For a number of years I have been coaching a couple of swim lanes at the mid-week club session. My group are usually already strong competent swimmers. When it's busy the role is primarily organising a worthwhile training session that will include some technique work. It provides little scope for giving individual attention. But I try to bring to the sessions the experience I have of being a triathlete - and that is a key point, as the focus of the group is preparation for a triathlon not for competing in a swimming gala (see Appendix 3).

It's important that people enjoy the session and feel they are getting something out of it. You have to plan to fill the hour in a way that keeps everyone moving while avoiding gridlock in the lanes. And we can't over-run as the water polo group who follow will be pulling away the lane ropes and setting up goalposts ready to begin their session. There was more to organising a coached training session than I had supposed.

Unconsciously I find the ethos of those I work with coming into my own coaching philosophy: encouraging effortless movement and symmetry, promoting relaxed effort as being more powerful, the purposeful mindset, making sure the core is switched on, getting comfortable with being uncomfortable and so on - all good themes that the group respond to.

Some interesting observations emerge. One is that a relatively big increase in effort can show surprisingly little difference in outcome. This emphasises how form and technique are so important; any slippage in these areas reduces the efficiency of the stroke and will slow you down.

Another observation is that although we all know about the importance of warming up, few appreciate what a good warm up entails. It's noticeable that the swimmers are often performing at their strongest when well into the second half of the session, perhaps after 40 or 45 minutes when the engines have been firing for a considerable time. When you point this out, it is definitely an eye opener. It's good to see people gaining in confidence and surprising themselves.

As a youngster I learned to swim in a salmon pool in the River Lyne in Peeblesshire. I seem to have come full circle to appreciate that there's something special about swimming in open water. It has a sense of freedom and adventure, the awareness that swimming is not merely a life skill but a means of travel, like walking and cycling. One of the most exhilarating things you can do is to wade into a loch and swim to the other side. And if the far side would be a long trek to reach by other means, that makes it more exhilarating still.

I only discovered this through triathlon. For years I had been swimming regularly at club sessions in an indoor pool without fully appreciating how one-dimensional it was. These sessions are still essential to maintain though, as the skills developed in the pool provide the attributes on which to build the skill sets required in open water.

I was 60 before I bought my first wetsuit so I could take part in triathlons with an open-water swim. Going along to the weekly club sessions at Loch Venachar over the summer months, I quickly realised how different and multi-dimensional it was.

Loch Venachar was a magnificent location; crystal clear water surrounded by hills and forests. At first I swam with a group keeping close to the shore, then after a few weeks I joined others who swam out to a small island.

This was where I first felt that sense of freedom. The island was little more than a pile of stones protruding from the water. At a 450m distance it was a fairly small speck that was even more difficult to see against a low evening sun. We would pull ourselves out of the water onto the stones to regroup before heading back again, aiming for one of the tall trees by the shore. Swimming across that stretch of water - the only sound the light rhythmic splashing of our strokes - was magical.

Open-water swimming developed a twin purpose for me:

training for triathlon and simply enjoying the profound pleasure of wild swimming.

The first realisation for me was that - without seeing tiles beneath the water - it's difficult to swim in a straight line. It's like swimming on your back in an outdoor pool looking at the sky and discovering you've turned ninety degrees. In an expanse of water you must keep looking up to check your direction, with some object or distant landmark to aim for.

Then there is a whole host of other variables. There's fresh water and salt water, calm water and choppy water, clear water and opaque water, the effects of wind and currents, swimming with a wetsuit and swimming without a wetsuit. On occasion there can be other surprises too, like the jellyfish in Denmark. And in a triathlon, you need to learn to swim with people around you, to survive the crowd and spot opportunities for using other swimmers to your advantage.

My personal classic is the 1.9km swim in Loch Tay for the Aberfeldy Middle Distance Triathlon, which is not actually held at Aberfeldy but at Kenmore. I've done this swim many times as part of a team. I admire those who do the whole event solo but I wouldn't contemplate it myself.

It is a big loch set in magnificent wild scenery. Because it is very deep, Loch Tay is always a few degrees cooler than elsewhere. Beneath you the water is dark, inky black, but when you see your outstretched hand below it's crystal clear. You can see the white stream of air bubbles from movement ahead. You can even read the small numbers on the timing chips attached to the ankles of swimmers around you.

Even in mid-August the water can feel chilly, rarely more than 13°C. I have always worn a thermal helmet under my swim cap and been glad of it.

Occasionally it has been flat calm, mirror smooth. But when there is a wind sweeping down the loch's 15-mile length, there will be a significant swell to contend with. Decisions need to be taken - whether to swim over the waves or try and slice through them. You can experience that disconcerting sensation of stroking thin air when straddling a trough.

I take comfort from knowing I am only swimming and I can give it my all. But most others will have a 90km bike ride and a 21km run still ahead of them when they leave the water.

In the maelstrom of a start wave with up to 300 swimmers it can be difficult to settle into a good position but the clear visibility in the water provides scope to move around. The closer you are to the person in front, the greater the drafting effect, but you should also be careful to avoid making contact. There's nothing more annoying than having your feet continually being tapped from behind. The drafting benefit works best if the swimmer in front is undisturbed.

The Loch Tay swim used to be a course of two laps but since 2013 it has become one large triangular lap with longer stretches of up to 700m between the buoys. The final side of the triangle is the critical part. Crossing the loch back to the jetty by the Crannog Centre - a landmark that blends into the adjacent countryside - you are aiming for a very distant buoy, often while swimming directly into a low dazzling sun. That's tricky at the best of times but if there is a wind the current will drag you to the left. And if your preferred side to breathe is to your right, when you open your mouth you're likely to take water, not air, on board.

Several times I've found that when I eventually spot the final buoy, it is way over to my right. So I've had to exercise even more effort against the current to take corrective action. I often wonder how the person in the lead manages to do it.

I say this swim is a personal classic because it's the longest competitive swim I do. With 35 to 40 minutes in the water, there is time to savour the experience and the challenge it presents. The single large triangle gives scale, the distance between each buoy allows you to settle and focus and the loch with its majestic surroundings conveys a feeling of being in big nature. After a taste of that - often quite literally - an indoor swim is never quite the same.

Seawater is more buoyant than inland water, so swimming in the sea with a wetsuit is about as buoyant as it gets. But you're less likely to have calm waters for a sea swim unless the course is contained within a sheltered area. When the water is opaque and you're unable to see your outstretched hand, the other swimmers are only visible when you look up. In that situation drafting is difficult and so you have to work much harder on your own.

I can't help reflecting on why the water should be so

opaque in the docks at Lisbon and Düsseldorf, the Danube at Budapest, the Serpentine in Hyde Park, the Marine Lake at Southport - which had rather too many waterfowl around for my liking on the day I was there. It's probably best not to think about it too much, just make sure none of it passes your lips!

At the other extreme, I've been in some dazzlingly clear water in an urban lake in Bratislava, in Lac Léman at Geneva and at Lausanne, Hawrelak Park in Edmonton, the sea off the Corniche in Abu Dhabi and many of the Scottish lochs. Given the choice, of course you would prefer to swim in these conditions. There is however, always the element of surprise. And sometimes you don't even realise you are being surprised.

After turning 65, I made the journey to Beijing for the World Age Group Championships. It was a memorable trip, the first and only time I have been to China and the event was staged at the same venue where the Olympic triathlon had been held three years before.

We swam in the Ming Tombs Reservoir with spectator stands stacked along the length of the dam. The weather was warm but it didn't seem quite so warm as to justify the water temperature announcement: 26°C. Wetsuits would not be permitted.

I was still relatively inexperienced at swimming in open water and in a race without a wetsuit I would be struggling. What kind of thermometer were they using? The evening before I had dipped in the water and it was definitely warm, strangely warm almost like a bath. But this was a significant patch of water nearly 10km in circumference.

The morning itself was wet with rather chill air. Because I was in a late start wave I had to wait around for a couple of hours in a marquee with puddles on the floor and no-where to sit down, getting steadily colder. Eventually, when the time came to start, it was a huge relief to get into the warm water, though I still couldn't fathom its temperature.

Some time later I looked up the name of the place where we stayed. It was called the Fengsahn Hotspring Resort. Perhaps a clue was in the name.

I didn't realise I was being surprised when I was at the ITU event in Abu Dhabi in 2017. The first part of the swim is in the yacht marina, before heading out into a sea channel for a few hundred metres to the transition area.

I was conscious that the distance felt longer than usual, especially as I was catching a number of tail-enders from the wave that started 10 minutes before. It seemed a long stretch from the second last buoy to the final one. My goggles had misted up and I took time to remove and rinse them rather than risk going astray.

Nevertheless I had a good swim, coming out of the water in about 30th place out of around 150 in my start wave, which was for all the M40+ categories. Studying the results in more detail afterwards, I noticed that my swim time was about five minutes slower than I would expect, although I considered it one of the better ones.

Many had taken considerably longer, some more than twice as long. And when I finished third in my age group, it was apparent that my encouraging result was all down to the swim time. Those who fell behind in the swim had never caught up. What was the explanation?

It turns out that in the second half of the swim, along the sea channel, we had been swimming against a strong tidal current. Many of the competitors had made very little headway against it. I hadn't even been aware of it at the time! But it all made sense afterwards.

On a similar theme, there was a strong current to contend with at the European Aquathlon Championships at Pontevedra in Spain, though this time it was evident to see. It's a wide river and standing on the bank you could see it flowing swiftly.

Our swim course was 1km in distance, up-river for 500m then back with the flow to the swim exit. We started out in the middle of the river lining up between two buoys. When I had watched earlier heats, I could see that some of the competitors were swimming quite hard to stay on the start line and one or two failed to make any progress when the hooter sounded. My plan to distribute effort evenly over the race had to be abandoned. Full effort would be required from the start if I were to reach the halfway point of the swim.

It was hard work, especially when I started to get knocked about by the arrival of the advance guard from the next heat.

I was pushed aside by the passing swarm only to move into the path of others. It was a relief to turn down-river but after all the bumping I didn't have the energy to take advantage of the easier ride. As I have alluded to before, in situations where I'm spent, I stay spent. It wasn't one of my better races but it was a memorable experience.

Several of my more memorable swims have come in aquathlons. I took part in my first championship aquathlon on my 70th birthday, as described in an earlier chapter. It was a wonderful experience, only possible because I improved my swimming technique during my late 60s.

Then the following year I took part in the corresponding event held in Bratislava. It was hot, sunny weather and the venue was on the outskirts of the city. I'd never been to Bratislava before; I had been a little put off by its reputation as a party destination. But we enjoyed the pleasant ambience of its interesting old town with no sign of visiting revellers.

The race started in a lake with crystal-clear water shimmering brightly in the sunshine. Its clarity was stunning, at odds with my expectations. All of us started together on the lakeside and ran into the water, heading straight out for about 250m before turning and coming back.

There was the customary exit, up the beach round a marker flag and back into the water for a second lap. It's hugely entertaining for the spectators but I find the beaching interlude takes that little bit extra out of you, making it more difficult to find a settled rhythm for the second half.

The two swimmers I'd been tracking were much sharper than me running back into the water. They were away and my contact with them was lost. I was left to work on my own, someone behind me taking advantage of tracking me and showing no interest in going ahead.

After front-loading my effort during the swim, the 5km run was always going to be difficult. And it was. Mike and Herbert were well in front but I managed to keep hold of third place. Though a satisfactory outcome, it was a less satisfying performance than the year before. That had felt like a much better race.

For its novelty, my most memorable swim so far occurred at the European Age Group Aquathlon Championships in Ibiza.

The decision regarding use of wetsuits was always going to be marginal. I was convinced they would be allowed given the circumstances. The race was starting in the late afternoon, arranged so that competitors would finish as the sun went down, taking advantage of what the locals claim to be some of the best sunsets in the Mediterranean. But the final decision was non-wetsuit.

Competitors were taken out to sea in ferryboats. One kilometre from the shore, you might easily have thought we were playing at pirates. A gangplank was pushed out from the stern and one at a time we walked its length and jumped into the swell. At least we weren't blindfolded.

The jump was around the height of my living room ceiling and it's a Victorian house. If I was thinking of changing my mind it was certainly too late.

In the rise and fall of the swell, the stronger swimmers in front were not visible for long. I settled into my own stroke with others who were swimming at my pace. I was now more confident swimming without a wetsuit than some years before and more proficient, but it was a challenge in these conditions. The distant buoy was only visible when cresting a wave.

It was quite an adventure and one that grows in the telling. Though somewhat off the pace, I thoroughly enjoyed it. And the run that followed did indeed finish in the orange glow of a setting sun.

In the summer months, when not otherwise involved in events, I attend weekly club sessions at Loch Venachar in the Trossachs. The sessions usually begin in June, although often it may be July before the water shows any sensation of warmth. Then by late August we're getting towards the end of the triathlon season and the evenings begin to close in. So our open water training season is fairly limited. But I did become much more accustomed to open water.

Loch Venachar is a sizable stretch of water, about four miles in length and aligned east-west. There doesn't have to be much wind for a swell to develop and the loch can present a range of conditions from flat calm to waves with white horses.

There I became comfortable swimming for up to 2km

in a wetsuit. We had some special evenings in the good summer of 2018 - warm sunshine, a pleasant water temperature and no midges, which is an unusual combination.

The clear sparkling water and magnificent setting surrounded by hills and forests, plus the quietness, are enchanting. One evening, a group of four or five of us out in the middle of the loch stopped to regroup. In complete silence, gently treading water, we were absolutely spellbound, the surrounding hills and forests bathed in a soft ethereal light.

There wasn't a sound. For a while no one spoke; all absorbed by the sensation of being where we were, just our heads above the water, caught in this magical scene. It was an experience to be treasured and one that only came about through training for triathlon.

Summer evening at Loch Venachar (page 81)

Continuing the weekly swim until the clocks changed - Loch
Lubnaig at the end of October (page 153)

Photo © Sarah Malcolm

Triathlon venue Beijing (page 76)

European Aquathlon Championships, Pontevedra, Spain 2019

Swimming against the current at Pontevedra

The transition zone can seem like a blurred forest of bikes. Work out beforehand a reliable way to recognise your position (page 25)

European Triathlon Championships 2018, Strathclyde Park,
Glasgow (page 120)

Photo © Ross Wood

Volunteers at a drinks station in Dubai

The blue carpet for the approach to the finish

Attracting media attention in Abu Dhabi (page 97)

A winning performance in 2019 (page 109)

Photo © ITU World Triathlon Abu Dhabi / Abu Dhabi Sports Council

Three generations completed their events at the Abu Dhabi Triathlon in 2018 - with grandson Alasdair and son-in-law Gareth

With Chris at the World Aquathlon Championships in Denmark 2018

Photo © Kim Ingleby

A podium team-finish for the family at the Aberfeldy Middle Distance Triathlon in 2018 - a swim to combine with son Ross on the bike and son-in-law Gareth running (page 73)

Scottish Triathlon Championships at Knockburn Loch, Banchory,
Aberdeenshire 2017

Swim exit in Denmark 2018 (page 68)

Lisbon 2016 - the best arrangements for a transition zone (page 118)

The transition 'shelter' (page 133)

Success from 'priority' races in 2018

Finishing at Lausanne 2019 (page 143)

Photo © FinisherPix®

"Events usually start around first light, swimming in the sea as the sun is rising." Al Hudayriat, Abu Dhabi

Photo © Gareth Manton

Eight

UAE ADVENTURES

"No public displays of nudity." I didn't have this intention in mind when I lined up for my first triathlon in the United Arab Emirates but it was prominently flagged as a no-no in the competitor information.

The only garment I might shed during the race would be my wetsuit - always assuming wetsuits were permitted. I'd be removing my helmet too at some point, but surely that wouldn't offend anyone? Come to think of it there would be a shoe change as well.

Such were the sensitivities around the introduction of triathlon to a viewing public in the UAE when I started taking part in events there in 2011.

I have to thank my younger daughter Kirsten for bringing a new dimension to my triathlon experiences when she and her husband Gareth went to live in the UAE for a couple of years. On an early visit I discovered that the first of the prestigious Abu Dhabi triathlons had been held shortly before and the finish was barely 200m from my daughter's flat.

So the following year I made sure a visit would coincide with the next event. Conveniently the organisers introduced a Sprint to run alongside the Long Course and the Short Course. Perfect. Considering the Short Course had a bike leg of 100km, the only feature that could justify its name was that it wasn't as long as the Long course, which had a bike leg of 200km.

The Sprint event was half the distance of the Short course and closer to what I was accustomed to. It had the conventional swim and run distances of 750m and 5km, separated by a bike ride of 50km rather than the usual 20km. That was do-able but it did appear to be a bike race bookended by a swim and a run. The extra distance on the bike would add around an hour to my usual racing time, increasing it to two and a half hours.

It's hot in the UAE in March. The longer courses started as soon as there was daylight but the starts for the Sprint came later, with my wave scheduled for 9am. By that time the air was already warm and rapidly getting warmer. And without any shade, I was wilting.

It came as a big relief to set off and get immersed in the cool water of the bay by the Emirates Palace. It is an amazing setting: white sand, calm turquoise water and a stunning backdrop.

The transitions at that time were more complicated than usual in order to avoid any inappropriate exposure of bare flesh. To ensure proper decorum a huge marquee was an integral part of the transition arrangements, laid out as an enormous cloakroom with rows of benches and coat-pegs.

We had each been given two drawstring bags to hang on our numbered peg, to contain all the equipment we would require during the event - bike shoes, running shoes, helmet, shades, sun hat and so on - and in which to deposit everything that would be discarded such as swim hat, goggles, wetsuit. Nothing was to be left on the benches or on the ground.

As all the removing and adding of clothes took place inside the marquee, onlookers then saw us emerge properly clad as we headed for the bike racks to get on our way. It all seemed very civilised and didn't appear to get in the way of an efficient transition; it was just a matter of adjusting usual routines to do things differently.

I had a good swim and finished quite well up in my start wave. Swimming, unlike cycling, was apparently not a strength amongst the participants - perhaps a reason for the disproportionately long bike courses.

My course of 50km went out and back on the main highway along the Corniche, over Saadiyat Bridge and towards Yas Island in the shape of an arc. Propelled by a following breeze I started fairly strongly, too strongly as it turned out, as I had a reality check when the road curved into the wind towards the turn.

It was hardly a surprise that the second half of the bike course, when the temperature rose to 35 degrees, became an increasing struggle. The run of 5km to finish off was flat, out and back on the tiled promenade - with no shade.

I don't remember much about the later stages but I do recall crossing the finish line and hearing an official ask if I was all right. I responded 'yes' on autopilot but they obviously knew better.

They took me to the medical tent to become a statistic on a bed with ice packs around me and quantities to drink. A classic case of dehydration and heat exhaustion. In due course I was released when my body temperature had returned to an acceptable level. But in spite of all the drama, I felt fine afterwards - apart from my legs, which were distinctly stiff.

It was a big learning experience - the need to prepare for and respect conditions that are way beyond those to which I'm accustomed.

Lasting images are of the pre-race pasta party and post-race banquet held on sultry evenings at the beach club of a splendid hotel - linen tablecloths, waiters with white gloves and a feast to match. All in all, the entire event was a difficult triathlon experience to beat.

My wife Chris and I wouldn't have thought of visiting Abu Dhabi had Kirsten and Gareth not moved there. But we made our first visit in early 2010, finding it a pleasant and family-friendly environment; day after day of cloudless blue skies, a ribbon of beaches extending along the Corniche for at least 8km with a promenade and cycle path running its full length. There are more green spaces than you might expect and plenty of colourful landscaping.

With the start of the Abu Dhabi adventures, my triathlon season began to split into two parts: races in the UAE at the beginning of the year and then the season at home which would run from around May to September.

Ten years on and the family is still there. Over that period I've made frequent visits in late autumn and early spring, taking part in events and sometimes training with the local club. It is a very agreeable winter destination. I can't speak about the summer but in winter it's hot. Events usually start around first light with swimming in the sea as the sun is rising. It's so different from home. In a Sprint triathlon it can be seriously warm by the time you are running and yet be finished by breakfast time.

Much has changed since my early visits. There are now events on many weekends over the period from November to March, with participation levels steadily increasing. There are relatively few older participants and I can be somewhat of a curiosity. Especially when the oldest age group is often for those aged 50 and over. At times it attracts some media attention - and the associated pressure of having to live up to expectations. It's something I'm unaccustomed to but it can be rather fun.

After my first triathlon in the UAE ended in the medical tent, I realised that more care was needed to handle the unfamiliar conditions. On returning home that year I sought advice from Ruth at the Scottish Institute of Sport. I needed to know how to plan nutrition and hydration. Her coping strategies for the quantities and timing of fluid to be taken helped me achieve a much more successful race in 2012.

Another year later, in March 2013, the race was also memorable but for different reasons. The big news was that Alistair and Jonny Brownlee, fresh from their Olympic triumphs at London 2012, would be taking part in the 'Short' race. Inevitably they attracted a crowd of onlookers when setting up their Boardman bikes in the transition area. And they showed extraordinary patience at being interrupted time and again to be photographed with an arm around a stranger's shoulders.

On race day it was almost 9.30am when I started and - as expected - the temperature was already hot. We lined up on the beach, about 200 of us in the wave, and ran into the sea. A brilliant sensation. The sea was warm but declared wetsuit legal so I wore mine, one of only a few who did. Fortunately I had been able to spend a few minutes keeping cool in the water before starting.

When I reached the transition tent, it was crowded. Much more so than the two previous years. The passageways between the rows of cloakroom rails and benches were narrow and we were all on top of each other.

The evening before, my visualisation exercise suggested I should remove the wetsuit before heading into the aisles and, once at my numbered spot, quickly stuff it into the bag, take the things I would need - helmet, shoes, shades - and carry them with me to put on where there was more space near the exit. This saved some time and helped to avoid the worst of the close quarter combat.

Now under my new regime, I was experimenting with the strategy for being 'in the moment', not thinking about what had gone before or what lay ahead, allowing myself to become cocooned fully engrossed in the present and unaffected by what other competitors were doing.

The bike course was conducive to this. Two laps of 25km out and back along the dual carriageway to Saadiyat Island, it had very little variation other than the gradual climb for about a kilometre going over Saadiyat Bridge twice on each lap and the dead turns every 12.5km.

I believe I made a good attempt at 'ITM', my best so far, managing to hold it for most of the bike course. However, my mindset was suddenly interrupted just after the turn on the first lap. A posse of motorcycle outriders swept past enclosing the Brownlees pedalling furiously. It was a long straight road but the Brownlees shot past and out of sight in no time. It was an eye-opener to see first hand the speed at which they ride a bike. I thought I was pedalling quite hard but compared with them I could have been standing still.

During the ride I consumed three TORQ gels and about 1200mls of fluid. Probably not quite enough. While the first 2km of the run were reasonably comfortable, the remaining

3km were completed in 'hanging-on' mode. But it was a sensible performance overall, the best of my early Abu Dhabi Triathlons - those with the 50km bike rides - clearing aside the memories of the medical tent drama in 2011.

Crossing the finish line I could see Alistair Brownlee, showered and changed, talking to people and looking relaxed. But then the Olympic champion came over and asked how my race had gone. What a moment. We spoke for a little while and I asked him about his race too. He and his brother are true ambassadors for the sport, generous in giving others such encounters to remember. And now I know what it feels like to be overtaken in a race by the Olympic champion.

Often, when I'm in the UAE, I go down to the beach on the Corniche before breakfast. The lifeguards are already there in their high chairs, every 50m or so, like tennis umpires. Many of them are from Sri Lanka. They are pleased to see someone and happy to talk - their alert, wiry and athletic appearance emanates an assuring presence.

Inside the breakwater, the sea is usually calm as a millpond. The water shimmers a deep blue and I wade into its cool tranquility, immersing myself with a dive and gliding back to the surface. Often I'm the only person in the water, but sometimes there may be one or two others. This section of the beach stretches for about 1.5km without interruption, with several areas of water roped-off for swimming similar to the one I am in.

I swim up and down for a while, practising sighting on

distant landmarks and then return to the beach to slip on a t-shirt, my shades, sun hat and running shoes. The upper part of the beach is level and has firm sand, raked flat every morning, perfect for running. It is totally even with just the right amount of 'give' for someone who likes cushioning. Muscles feel so much looser in the warmth; there's a fluency and at times I'm able to stretch out my legs and feel like a runner in a way that doesn't happen back at home where beneath the protective layers, some stiffness is seldom far away.

But this is pure exhilaration. Leaving my bag beside the umpire's chair, I head to the near end of the beach, turn and run its full length to the far end and back before stopping, perhaps a little over 3km.

There are security guards around who sit on low chairs, sometimes in the shade of an umpire's chair or further up the beach. But there's hardly anyone on the beach this morning and little for the security men to do. One of them is strolling up and down close to where I've stopped.

When I saw him earlier he had been sitting on his chair and we'd exchanged an acknowledgement. This time he was pleased to chat. He said he had watched me running and thought I looked comfortable, so I thanked him for this positive assessment. Then he went on to ask what distance I had run because he'd timed me. I explained that I had been to the far end of the beach and back - what would that be? It was quite a distance, he thought.

We chatted for a while. He was from Uganda and would soon be returning home having spent two years in Abu Dhabi. He shared interesting insight into how he found living and working here. And he observed that coming from Scotland I was from the same part of the world as Andy Murray.

I mentioned my admiration for John Akii-Bua and it delighted him that I knew of the 400m hurdler who was the first Olympic champion to come from his country, winning gold at Munich in 1972. He had been fortunate to be around just before Ed Moses arrived on the scene to make the event his own for the next decade. I remembered Akii-Bua from 1970 when I was a member of the volunteer team at the Commonwealth Games in Edinburgh, putting the hurdles out on the track. He had finished fourth then.

I have no doubt my friend the security guard would be telling others about his encounter with a silver-haired gent who looked comfortable running on the beach. Like the lifeguards from Sri Lanka, he was baffled that a retired person should be doing this sort of thing. It didn't happen where he came from.

Because roads are wide, with fast-moving traffic, it's much more difficult to find suitable places to cycle in Abu Dhabi. But Gareth introduced me to midweek cycling at the Yas Marina motor racing circuit. The F1 racetrack is open one evening each week for cycling and running under the floodlights. We gather at one of the pit lanes and cyclists ride anticlockwise on the track while runners go clockwise on the outside apron.

The air is warm and sultry and there's music playing over the speakers. It is a special atmosphere cycling past the huge spectator stands. The track surface is so smooth, yet feels adhesive when cornering. Over the 5.5km circuit there is a hill, some intricate sections with 90-degree bends and there's also a hairpin. You have to slow down for the corners riding a bike. Imagine what it must be like when approaching at the speed of a racing car.

I didn't realise how close Abu Dhabi and Dubai are to each other - less than an hour and a half's drive between them - and since they both sprawl across the landscape, their outer edges are not very far apart. The Yas Marina Circuit is situated on the Dubai side of Abu Dhabi and here people come from both cities for an evening of cycling.

Over the time I have been going, numbers attending have increased significantly and rules for etiquette on the track have had to be introduced to separate the recreational from the serious. They've also needed to limit the number of bikes in a train.

The F1 track is the location of the TriYas triathlon, usually held in late February each year, shortly before the Abu Dhabi Triathlon. I started taking part in this event in 2015 as it was a good opportunity for a practise outing in race mode and warm conditions in preparation for the main Abu Dhabi race. But as it turned out, TriYas was an excellent event to do in its own right and I usually aim to arrange a visit to span both events.

There is no early morning start at TriYas; it begins in the heat of late afternoon. Swimming is in the marina amongst the moored yachts, while the transition area is appropriately in the pit lane. Once we set out on our bikes, we follow the route taken by the racing cars when they leave the pits, down into a tunnel under the track and up on the other side to join the circuit. The timing is arranged so that darkness falls during the race and we finish under the floodlights.

Having trained on the track, it's exhilarating knowing the circuit, cycling four laps in race mode. I have to be careful not to get carried away by the occasion on my first lap. I use the Garmin to note my lap times, trying to keep them even-paced. I've improved in this regard since the first time I did this race.

When Abu Dhabi was added to the ITU World Triathlon Series programme in 2015, the World Series event superseded the original Abu Dhabi triathlon. Under different management, the focus was on the elite men's and women's races that attract global attention. The associated age group events then became conventional Sprint, Standard and Middle Distance races, with more familiar lengths for the bike courses. In effect there was a clean break between 2014 and 2015, with a new location for the start and finish on the other side of the breakwater near the Sailing & Yacht Club by Marina Mall, and making full use of the classic images of the city backdrop and the Corniche.

Perhaps lack of space at that venue led to a further change, as in 2017 it moved away from the city to the motor-racing venue at Yas Marina Circuit (YMC). This may be more suitable logistically but it is at the expense of losing the iconic images of the city and the seafront. I have to say I prefer the original location in the heart of the city with all the action along the Corniche. It feels much more isolated at Yas.

As there is a full programme of events around Abu Dhabi and Dubai from October through to March, I keep alert for other races that might be included during visits. Although most of the participants are non-native to the region, considerable numbers participate.

One event that has become a favourite is the JLL Triathlon Series held at the Jebel Ali Resort in Dubai.

It's still dark as we set up our bikes for transition in the hotel car park - competitors are advised to bring a torch - before starting at sunrise with a swim in the marina. I like the bike course - two laps mixing fast stretches, speed bumps to be negotiated and some tight corners. Then we run our 5km out and back along the seafront. It's a compact race in a beautiful setting.

Then it finishes off in the epitome of style: a magnificent breakfast in the open-air, chefs cooking to our specifications, and we feast while the presentations take place in a setting that would befit any wedding reception. It's a different world and I remind myself that it's one I've encountered only through participating in my sport.

I continued taking part in the Abu Dhabi Triathlon each year, a highlight of the early season that is motivating over the winter months. In 2019 it was my ninth time of taking part in the event, now in its third year out of town at the Yas Marina motor racing track.

On this occasion the start of my race was scheduled for the early afternoon. It's hot in the UAE in March, and a 2pm start is at the hottest time of the day. I had been introduced to the reversal technique before and this was a situation ideally suited to such an approach. Kim and I talked about how I might apply it in earnest. I am not accustomed to a hot climate, let alone engaging in physical activity in the heat of the day, so it would be even more imperative than ever to respect the heat.

A series of questions was posed for me to consider. How did I want to look and feel after I finished? How did I want to feel during the run? And so on, working backwards - at the start of the run, during the bike ride, setting out on the bike and at each stage right back to the period before the start. So I set about thinking it through and writing down my thoughts, working back from immediately after the finish of the race when I would be "upright, composed, tired and satisfied".

It was an interesting exercise. Writing everything down brought a focus on the need to be economical in terms of energy output at every stage of the race. I noticed I gained confidence by believing it was a plan that could lead to finishing respectably without being in distress.

To my surprise, on race morning it was announced that wetsuits would be permitted. A mixed blessing. I'm always pleased to hear that wetsuits are allowed, though in this situation the time spent between putting on the wetsuit and getting into the water can be a challenge. But there was never any doubt: I would wear my wetsuit.

Often before a race I think I have plenty of time only to end up rushing to the start line. This time I had a schedule for the two-hour period between transition closing and my wave starting. It allowed for a period of relaxed reading in a cool corner of the vast spectator stands, topping up with some energy nutrition, wetsuit and body lubrication, putting on the lower half of the wetsuit, going to the bag drop and so on. I arrived at the holding pen unhurried and on cue.

Waiting in the start pen in a wetsuit without shade was gruelling. I ended up pouring the bottles of water we were given down the neck of the wetsuit to stop myself from overheating while we shuffled along the quayside towards the starting point.

We had a rolling start, stepping forward randomly four at a time every five seconds to set off running down the ramp, over the timing mat and launching into the water. At a practical level it makes sense as the channel is narrow until clear of the yachts and it stops a lot of the drafting, but those with competitive aspirations are less happy as they don't know where they stand when it comes to racing it out near the end. However, my objective was a BRP: the focus was entirely on myself, others could take care of themselves.

It was a relief to get into the water. The first thing I had to do was to sort my goggles, which had slipped down onto my cheeks after the running dive into the water.

There was little drafting opportunity during the swim. We seemed quite spread out. Following the strategy gave me a feeling of security. I settled into a calm positive rhythm and enjoyed the coolness of the water.

On completion of the swim we arrived at a big transition area, perhaps more than 150m long.

I find it awkward running on a hard surface in bare feet without proper orthotic support, which makes me relatively slow when there is a large transition zone. But we had been free to choose where we racked our bikes. Most were clustered close to where we had first entered on arrival, but I chose to rack mine near the exit from the swim because that would give me the shortest distance to run barefoot.

The wetsuit peeled off effortlessly with the magic TriSlide lubricating spray. I tried to put on my bike shoes while standing but it wasn't happening so I sat down instead. Nevertheless it felt a fairly efficient transition overall.

I was familiar with the bike course - a lot of tight corners and dead turns in the first half followed by fewer interruptions in the second half. I could have cycled with more effort, especially into the stiff breeze, but I disciplined myself to keep to the plan and be as economical as possible, focusing on the end point. That was wise, and it was gratifying to see afterwards that my time for the bike course still began with a three. Just.

In terms of the strategy I was in exactly the right place when I started the run. I felt comfortable and focused, and knew that I would be able to hold my pace the whole way. I passed a number of people - when normally it would be few or none - and several were struggling to keep going. I enjoyed focusing on relaxed comfortable running, taking plenty of water and pouring most of it over my head and shoulders, and kept up a steady pace.

The second half remained strong and I was able to finish with that deeply satisfying feeling of having given it every-thing - just as envisaged in the original plan. The split times confirmed what I felt - I started the run in 5th place in the 'M60+' category and finished third.

I had been listed as one of 11 in the oldest category, which was 60+. However, by the time the presentations were made, the category had become 60-69 and I was rather surprised to be announced as the winner of M70+.

I think I would have preferred to be in third place on a full podium than alone on the top step of an otherwise empty one. But I was certainly very pleased with how I had performed. There was a good plan, it was appropriate for the circumstances, and I stuck to it. I couldn't have done any better, I finished the way I wanted to and it was a BRP. To have been 137th overall out of 368 finishers in my fourth season of the 70+ age group was a satisfying outcome. It confirmed to me the value of not merely having a well thought through plan, but also sticking to it.

Nine

ON THE BIKE

I'm trying to ride at an even pace - or perhaps I should say an even effort level. My approach is different from what it was before. I used to ride as hard as I could and then let the run take care of itself but I've learned to be a bit smarter. Now my mindset is to have the best bike ride to give me the best running performance. It's a deliberately positive mindset. I'm not holding myself back but focused on preparing for the next part of the race. That's important to me because something else I've realised is that no longer do I have the ability to recover in-race from being in oxygen debt. If I'm spent I stay spent, which besides hindering overall performance reduces the enjoyment.

It was a good plan to drive round the course the evening before. I feel relaxed as I pedal steadily uphill, knowing it will continue that way for the first 10km. I also know that the gradient is steepest just before the top and I enjoy a psychological boost from passing some riders on that final section. The second half of the course continues in a sweeping loop through the Bedfordshire countryside back down to the valley with the final 2km on flat roads into a slight wind.

As it turns out, my time for the bike course is better than usual relative to my age group peers. Why is that? The familiarisation gained the evening before definitely helped. I knew what would be involved and paced myself appropriately. And unlike some previous rides, I did not allow my concentration to slip in the final 2km. Also, for some unknown reason I decided to inflate my tyres to 110psi whereas normally they would be inflated to 100psi. Would that have made a difference? Several things to think about.

At least I have avoided the dilemma faced by some enthusiasts: which bike to ride or which set of wheels to use. There are disc wheels, deep-rim wheels, wheels with many spokes and ones with hardly any. Some have flat spokes, others round. And so it goes on. The myriad varieties all have qualities for suiting a particular purpose. At most my choice is between a road bike and a time trial bike; each has only one set of wheels. I will normally use the time trial bike for a sprint triathlon unless the course is particularly hilly or intricate, in which case the road bike might be more suitable.

I remember being at the world age group championships in Chicago when a storm was forecast and the organisers announced that disc wheels would not be allowed. The announcement caused another storm. Many competitors had only brought a disc wheel with them. They had to seek out others who could lend them a suitable rear wheel. I had assumed Chicago would be windy because of its name as the "Windy City". However, I later learned the origin of the name was to do with a reputation for long-winded politicians.

As the bike distance for the sprint triathlon is normally 20km - around 40 minutes - my training rides are often an hour's duration and seldom more than 90 minutes. But for a few years now I have been in the habit of joining a weekly group for a two-hour ride with a coffee-shop finish. With the addition of the distance to and from the meeting place it comes to nearly two and a half hours of riding. Although styled as a 'recovery' ride and taken at a considerate pace, I have found the added distance helpful for improving cycling endurance.

Some of the group are from the local bike club and I've learned from being with them and observing how they ride: the stable upper body when working on the hills and their generally higher leg cadence. Apparently cadence is a personal thing but it is significant that the pure cyclists tend to ride with a higher cadence. I noticed smaller details too: whether they had the legs of their shades inside or outside the helmet strap. That affects how easily they come off in unplanned circumstances.

Power meters and heart rate monitors have never been part of my scene. The Garmin is my only concession to technology for training and racing. I have it programmed to display the four pieces of information I find useful: my speed (kph), cadence (rpm), distance travelled (km) and elapsed cycling time. Some of my contemporaries still work in miles but race distances are in kilometres - and I must say the bigger numbers look better.

As drafting other competitors in a triathlon event is not usually permitted, concentration is important. A lapse can allow your pace to drop without realising. An eye needs to be kept on the bike computer to remain alert to a drop in speed or cadence from what you would expect to see. It took me some time to have strategies to counter this - but they did make a difference.

As I have mentioned, about half of the time in a triathlon is spent cycling; it's not far off the combined time spent swimming and running. That means it has a significant influence on the overall outcome. Cycling differs from the other disciplines in its range of speeds. Unless the course is flat and windless there will be periods when you are going at more than twice the speed you may be doing at other times. It's clear that the time spent cycling at slow speeds has the greatest impact on the overall time taken.

I've talked about my need to distribute effort efficiently to avoid straying into the zone from which it is difficult to recover - where the second wind that previously came on cue no longer arrives. So the most important part of the race to reconnoitre, as far as I'm concerned, is the bike course. To optimise my average speed I will try and put more effort into the parts that will be slower - uphill or into the wind - and coast more on the quicker sections. And a good streamlined position helps significantly.

Memorable images spring to mind from bike courses at age group championships held abroad. In my first year of being with the GB age group team, we were in Hamburg. Officials on motorbikes were policing the drafting rules rigorously. Those judged to be in breach had to stop, dismount the bike and hold it above their head before being permitted to continue. For those riding past it was of course hilarious to see a competitor at the side of the road with bike held aloft, humiliated and fizzing with rage.

At one point on my second lap, three riders swept past me on each other's wheels. For a brief moment I was tempted to try and hang on but my hesitation was enough for them to get away from me. However, a short time later I passed one of them at the side of the road with bike held high and looking incandescent. It was difficult to resist the urge to give him a wave. It's the only time I have come across this particular penalty for drafting; normally there's no drama, just a straightforward time penalty.

There's another vivid memory from Chicago. I've mentioned the importance I attach to a bike course recce, but a significant part of the bike route was on busy highways that were only closed for the race days. Competitors were not allowed to cycle on them beforehand. We had been warned that the road surface was poor in places but I did not realise just how poor it would turn out to be. It was narrower than the rest of the course and quite dangerous - paving with ill-fitting joints and a lot of potholes.

The first hint of trouble on the road ahead was the sight of water bottles rolling around, followed by random bike parts. Although the worst of the fixed hazards were marked with yellow spray paint you couldn't always spot them in good time. Swerving to avoid one could land you in the path of another. There were a lot of bikes on the course and a lot of sudden swerving going on. Twice I thought I would puncture when hitting potholes or bike debris I couldn't avoid but fortunately I didn't. Very fortunately, because similar hits at home had resulted in a flat tyre.

By the second lap I knew what was involved, could anticipate better and was flip-jumping on the tri bars at 35kph, not something I had thought to practise or would recommend. Rather scary, actually. At a world championship you expect to find courses of the best quality. This was an unexpected nightmare, undoubtedly the worst road surface I've encountered for a triathlon race.

My particular anxiety about the potholes stemmed from an occurrence only a few weeks before, training along a country road. There had been a big jolt and within 50 metres the front tyre was flat. Being warm and dry it wasn't too much trouble to fit a new inner tube and inflate the tyre again and then I was on my way once more. But no sooner was I back on the bike than I realised the rear tyre was also flat. And I'd just used the only spare inner tube I had with me.

What to do? It was a quiet road with nothing much about

but I noticed a police car waiting by the verge about 200m away in the direction from which I had just come. How it came to be there I don't know. I gave a forlorn wave and shortly it began to move towards me. On explaining my predicament the two officers asked me where I was going. As they were about to head back to Stirling they said they would take me home and they managed to fit both the bike and myself into the back of their car. What amazing good fortune. After that I always took the precaution of carrying two spare inner tubes.

Potholes aside, Chicago left one abiding memory that had nothing to do with the triathlon. Chris and I managed to get tickets for a concert at the opening weekend of the Chicago Symphony Orchestra's 125th anniversary season. It started at 7pm in the evening, leaving just enough time to see the leaders of the men's elite race finishing. We made our way quickly to the concert hall a block away from the race venue and arrived to find a red carpet on the pavement - by that I mean the sidewalk - and people in ball gowns and black ties. Despite having tidied ourselves up beforehand, at best it was as reasonably presentable triathlon spectators that we snuck stealthily to our seats just before seven.

It was a fantastic concert, and inspirational to see and hear one of the world's famous orchestras perform familiar works. But the most memorable part came right at the start. The concert began with the playing of the national anthem, orchestra and audience all standing. To experience the Stars and Stripes being performed by a full-strength symphony orchestra accompanied by a capacity audience, all with hand on heart and in full voice was sensational. The hairs on the backs of our necks were tingling. It absolutely took our breath away.

The lack of opportunity for a course recce at Chicago clearly had some bearing on the European Age Group Championships at Lisbon the following year. Once again the course was on a major highway and we would have no opportunity to cycle the bike course before race day. But I believe pressure was brought to bear in order to provide an opportunity, since we were told that the police would allow everyone to ride the course as a group the morning before the race.

A huge peloton of several hundred riders assembled at the appointed time and set off with police escort and motorcycle outriders leading us round the 20km route at a smart pace, blue lights flashing and sirens sounding. Brilliant! All over in a blur. I needed to pedal hard to keep up and hoped I would be able to do as well in the race without the benefit of being sucked along in a big pack.

In terms of the pre-start, transition area and post-finish arrangements, the venue at Lisbon was one of the best I have come across. An arena and spacious sports hall provided both a calm and sheltered area for final preparations close to the start and a comfortable recovery area after the finish with our bags on hand. The transition area was probably the only one I've experienced that had a roof. A covered space like a huge carport between two buildings, open on two sides giving protection from sun or rain.

It was at Lisbon that I had my first brush with drafting. I was warned, but not penalised, by a passing official on a motorcycle. I was convinced I wasn't drafting. Perhaps that's what everyone says, but a number of people reported a similar experience from what we reckoned was an over-zealous outrider who seemed to enjoy blowing his whistle. I was instructed to increase my distance from the rider in front, which, going into a strong wind, meant losing all my momentum.

And there was a sequel just one week later. In a qualifying race back home for the following year's championships at Düsseldorf I was penalised two minutes for drafting - without knowing anything about it at the time. It was only apparent when looking at the results afterwards. At least a number of competitors had been similarly penalised. Fortunately, despite the time penalty, my result had sufficient headroom to secure qualification for the Euros in 2017.

These two incidents gave me a wake-up call to be more careful. Two minutes is the time I take to cover about a kilometre on a bike. It would be careless to risk throwing that distance away in an important event.

I am not a cyclist in the sense that many triathletes are or certainly most of my triathlon peers are. As a teenager I cycled to school every day, perhaps a distance of about two miles. But 20 years passed before I was back on a bike, commuting three miles to work. So I was cycling regularly over short-ish distances without breaking sweat. When it came to dabbling in triathlon my background as a runner enabled me to keep up a good enough rate turning the pedals to produce respectable bike times - but they were not the times you would expect of someone you would call a cyclist. Only after turning to triathlon more seriously in my 60s and upgrading to a proper road bike did I give any real attention to cycling.

In 2018, when I was in my third year of the 70-74 age group, the European championships were held at Strathclyde Park near Glasgow, the venue for the triathlon events at the 2014 Commonwealth Games. However, my journey to Glasgow had to begin the year before.

You can't just turn up to these championships. First you have to qualify and that means being sufficiently alert to take part in one of the qualifying races a year in advance. That took me to Southport 15 months beforehand, where fortunately qualification was secured. Having travelled abroad to these championships over the years, I couldn't miss them when they were being held less than an hour's drive from home.

Having qualified, I made a point of getting to know the bike course. On the hilly side of undulating, the middle part of the course weaves through wooded parkland and the lack of distinctive features makes it difficult to recognise where you are on the course. It took several visits before being confident that I understood the course and could recognise each part of it, where the dips and the inclines came and where I was in relation to them. I would work on the inclines, know which gear to be in and what cadence to hold.

And when coasting on the downhill sections I knew at what point to apply the additional momentum that would take me well into the next rise. Perhaps all that comes naturally to the experienced cyclist.

On my final visit I did a full practice session, cycling the three laps and timing each one. Having ridden each lap slightly quicker than the previous one, I then ran for 15 minutes along the loch-side to see how it felt. Running didn't feel too bad in spite of having been cycling at quite a high intensity. This gave me encouragement that when it came to the day, the 5km run should be manageable. But the most important effect was to give me greater confidence going into the race, feeling that I was well prepared and knowing exactly what I was going to do.

On race day I noted an interesting adrenaline effect. My first lap on the bike course was quicker than my fastest lap in practice, then the second lap was quicker than the first and the third one quicker again. And to follow I had a competent run, finishing in 5th place. It was an encouraging outcome for my third year in the 70-74 age group, especially compared with finishing 8th at Lisbon in my first year and then 6th at Düsseldorf in my second year. Though my competitors are no doubt different each time, I'm content to count that as progress.

Ten

SECOND TRANSITION

I can see the dismount line ahead. An official in a high-vis jacket is waving a flag and pointing to the red line on the ground. There was a warning sign 100m before, and two more signs are positioned in front of the line. You can't miss it - or at the very least there would be no excuse for missing it. I slow down, almost to a standstill, swing my left leg over the saddle and hop to the ground a few feet before the line.

The upper part of my right hamstring just below the gluteal is feeling a little tight, as it often does on completion of a triathlon bike ride, so I run carefully over the timing mat and into T2. There are several long rows of racking in the extensive transition area. But having rehearsed thoroughly when setting up, I turn confidently into mine. I start counting my steps. On cue, after 20, I recognise the small dark patch on the tarmac and know that just four paces further on should be my spot. Yes, I can see my running shoes and spare water bottle. Pushing the bike nose first into the gap, I hook the brake levers over the rail.

I'm in Switzerland and that was a much more efficient execution than one I recall from a championship event several years before when instead of checking the ground I'd scanned the numbers on the rail waiting for mine to resonate, only to realise with the end of the row approaching that I couldn't actually remember my five-digit race number - which at that point was on my back. I needed to retrace my steps. A valuable learning point had been taken on board which I successfully acted upon today.

I unfasten my helmet - no problems with cold fingers in these warm conditions - and I manage to remain on my feet while removing cycling shoes and transferring into running shoes. It sounds simple, but I'm breathing quite hard, at times needing to keep one hand on the bike for some support.

I find it helps to spray lubrication into the shoes beforehand. Otherwise any moisture, whether from swimming, weather or sweat, will cause a sock-less foot to stick when trying to insert it into the shoe. You need to be able to plant feet quickly and cleanly in the shoes without wrinkling insoles or leaving a toe on the outside. And I need good balance to avoid having to hop about on one leg while trying to put a shoe on the other foot.

A short tug tightens my lace toggles and then I continue to the far end of the row, running slowly to start with. My legs are still adjusting from cycling and I need to stay alert to ensure I head the correct way for the 'run exit'. By the time I exit the transition zone, I reckon I have covered about 400m since I entered with my bike. As I cross the timing mat my legs are finally showing signs of switching into running mode and functioning properly.

The second transition, T2, from bike to run, should be relatively straightforward. And with a clear head it is. But even the most straightforward of procedures can be a mine-field in a state of haste and short on oxygen. And I have a habit of managing to do inexplicable things.

Before now I've spent time hurrying to put on shoes that weren't mine. Fortunately I have large feet and didn't succeed. Another time I believed the way to stop myself from fading towards the end of the run would be to take an energy gel around half way. In order to remember the gel I propped it up in the heel of my running shoe, ready to pick up in T2 and slip into my back pocket. However, I didn't remember it until I was a couple of strides into my run and felt a sticky explosion inside my left shoe.

I've had many inexplicable incidents and although I take trouble to avoid making the same errors, new opportunities continue to arise. I have to hang a health warning over T2: don't drop your guard. If you stay alert, it's possible to surprise yourself and I've had some good efforts. I could just do with having more of them.

Do seconds matter? They matter more to me now than they did before, especially those that are lost unnecessarily. The needless waste of several seconds is an intrusion into momentum. I've done the maths. By wasting 10 seconds in T2 - something easily done - the person who was previously beside me is more than 30 metres ahead when I set out on the run. Seeing it in that light helps to focus the mind.

I'm told that I am capable of surprising myself. But I've only been truly aware of this happening once. It was at an age group qualification event at Nottingham, a prestigious venue with a big-race atmosphere. The centrepiece is the 2,000m long regatta lake of the National Watersports Centre at Holme Pierrepont. We swim in the lake, cycle four laps on the dead-flat roadway that encircles it, then run one lap in the opposite direction to the way we have cycled. My race plan included a focus on good transitions and a serious attempt at injecting effort into the second half of the run in order to counter my tendency to fade in the later stages. Much to think about.

About halfway round the first lap of the bike course I noticed I was in the vicinity of others I had never been alongside before, people who would be out of the water before me and then move further out of sight on the bike. Comfortable and confident, I was keeping up with them - not drafting of course, though at this venue there are so many competitors it is impossible to stay apart. The best you can do is to look as though you're trying not to draft. When a competitor - let's call him Robert, for convenience - who would eventually finish right up at the sharp end in my age group, overtook me after two laps I found it easy to stay with him into the strong wind and continue tailing him at a discreet distance.

Well, as T2 was approaching, Robert started freewheeling to unfasten his shoes; so I went past him and pressed on to the dismount line. And I did a superb transition, one of my best for T2. I had the unusual experience of finding my stretch of the rail empty, no bikes there yet. Bike shoes were removed in a flash this time, running shoes on and away. And I felt comfortable running at my usual pace. I became aware that I was surprising myself. It was a sensation I'd not experienced before and I was enjoying it. Just to make sure I wasn't dreaming, I even said out loud, "I'm surprising myself." I was at least 500m into the run before Robert came past - and he's a significantly quicker runner than I am.

The final piece of the jigsaw was to take an energy gel when I reached the far end of the lake, washing it down at the water station shortly afterwards. Then, perhaps a kilometre later and without any prior warning, I 'hit the wall'. My legs had gone and there was still about 1500m to the finish. I had to walk for a bit, then jog for a bit and walk again, and so on to the finish. But afterwards I felt absolutely fine. My run time was about two minutes slower than it might otherwise have been. In spite of the inexplicable ending, I still had a result I would have gladly settled for before the start. It was an extreme performance, with the first 90% going supremely well only for the wheels to come off in the final 1500m.

I never fathomed how I came to surprise myself like that but I must have hit some sweet spot that has since remained elusive. The fade at the end happened to me in a number of events around that time, though not in quite such a dramatic fashion. I eventually attributed this to the energy gels - they were a problem not the solution - and have since found it much more effective not to consume any energy products during a sprint triathlon.

Returning to Robert and T2, I was able to deduce from the split times that I had entered T2 four seconds ahead of him. This suggests the process of removing his feet from the bike shoes on the move added about six seconds to his bike time. And my time for T2 was, surprisingly, 10 seconds better than his. That means I gained 16 seconds on someone who kept his shoes fastened to the pedals. It confirmed something for me: there's no need to change my routine for T2. I just need to execute it consistently and well.

Eleven

CHAMPIONSHIP JOURNEY

It's lunchtime on Thursday and I'm having my final swim before travelling to England on Saturday. Conditions at Loch Venachar are amazingly hot, the water like a mill-pond. Four of us swim to the island, taking a loop round two of the sailing buoys back to the shore. I come up out of the water and put on a t-shirt. It's so pleasant to not have to think about keeping warm. Absolutely continental. After weeks of an unbroken heat wave, the water level is lower than I'd ever seen it.

This was the start of my journey to Lausanne for the World Age Group Championships that would take place in a little over a year's time. Taking part in European or World age group championships is not merely a matter of choosing. Participation has to be earned. Competitors are entered by their respective national federations - British Triathlon in my case - so long as they qualify in specified races held the year before.

I needed to place in the first four in my age group in at least one of three events in 2018 designated as qualifiers for Lausanne 2019. I was going to the third and final qualifier at Redcar on Teesside. Part of the attraction of going to Lausanne would be meeting up again with some of our Swiss orienteering friends. But I was feeling a little pressure. All my eggs were in one basket; there would be no further opportunity.

On reaching Redcar on Saturday evening, the storm that inevitably follows such a prolonged period of hot weather had arrived. And by the time I had driven round the bike course there was a message from the organisers saying that the sea swim might be cancelled. If so they would substitute it with a 2.5km run. Not the most welcome news. However, a final decision would be taken on the day.

It was windy and wild in the morning - 40mph gusts - with frequent heavy showers. The organisers had problems trying to secure race buoys in a heavy swell. They declared the swim to be on, and then off, then on again - all within the hour before the race started. Eventually we were told that two buoys had been secured and that would be sufficient to proceed. So the swim went ahead in fairly rough conditions with the water temperature declared as 14 degrees - it's the North Sea after all.

I was insufficiently prepared for adverse weather conditions. Being late July and leaving home in a heat wave I hadn't thought to take gloves or suitable protective garments for wearing on the bike. Fortunately, despite the wild conditions, it wasn't particularly cold.

The preparation I had done for the event helped me to stay thoroughly 'present'. All the uncertainties prior to the start combined with the challenging conditions could easily have been dispiriting and left me wondering why on earth I was doing this. But I kept a firm focus. And everything was fine once my start wave set off to run down the beach and into the sea.

We swam a short distance out to the first buoy then turned to continue parallel to the shore for the remaining distance. The water was choppy but in spite of the strong gusts it wasn't as rough as I was expecting. Perhaps as the wind was blowing away from the shore it prevented a bigger swell. The distance was certainly less than 750m judging by the swim times, which included running a considerable distance from the shoreline at low tide up the beach to the promenade and on further to the transition zone. But my swim went well and my T1 transition was good - the TriSlide spray really is magic. My wetsuit almost fell off when unzipped.

It was going to be my first experience of a draft legal bike ride, as the championships in Lausanne would be. I enjoyed that aspect, staying alert and ready to grasp opportunities, considering how to apply swim-drafting techniques to the bike ride. I was lucky too. On each of the four laps I managed to sit on a wheel during the long section into the teeth of the wind. The road bike felt light and manoeuvrable compared with the TT bike. I learned quickly that when drafting another bike at close quarters in lashing rain you have to keep your mouth closed and try to breathe through your nose - not easy when gasping for breath.

There was much buffeting on the run. At times it was difficult to put one foot in front of the other going into the wind along the promenade. At least there was no fading in the later stages; the policy of taking no fuel during a race, apart from water, has solved this particular issue.

Age groups are often clustered in transition areas. When arriving at T1 after the swim you can see how many bikes are still there and how many have gone. There is no finer sight than returning to T2 and finding the adjacent rails looking bare - a rare occurrence to be savoured, as often there may be plenty of bikes and one of the gaps will have your number on it. But this time the age groups were not clustered; it appeared to be a completely random arrangement. During the race I had no idea how I might be faring in comparison with others in my age group and I wasn't much the wiser on finishing.

However, I thought I'd had a good race - certainly a BRP for the conditions on the day. My strategy had been to keep momentum and flow from start to finish and I felt I achieved that. My swim and transitions had been sharp and I'd kept my mind on the task during the bike and run. And actually, I'd enjoyed it. I didn't hang about afterwards, just collected my gear and retreated to the shelter of the car. After sorting myself out I headed north. It turned out that I was the first finisher in M70: mission accomplished. I can't imagine how I would have felt if it hadn't been.

Conditions that day at Redcar were exceptional. I went, kept my blinkers firmly on, did the event and came away. It's only in retrospect that I appreciate how heroic the organisers and volunteers must have been. I realised that winter can occur on any day of the year, even when least expected. I knew that before, but now I have to remember I know it and always be prepared. If the air temperature had been just a little cooler, I would have needed protective gear.

It brought home to me that I should work out a better way of trying to keep shoes dry in bad weather when you are not allowed to have any bags, boxes or protective covers beside your bike in the transition area - only the kit you will be using during the race. It's not pleasant putting on saturated cycling and running shoes, particularly running shoes that have become heavy and will squelch with every step. On returning home I devised a 'shelter', placing the shoes with soles facing upwards, cycling shoes on top of running shoes, and wedged firmly in position between two water bottles (which are considered kit). I've used the arrangement successfully in wet weather several times since then.

I like the system of qualification. The criteria are straightforward. You know what is required. It means there are journeys to embark on for reaching European and World age group championships, which become a project. And if you can get there you know your presence is worthy.

The qualifying process has taken me to events beyond my local sphere that I wouldn't normally go to: Nottingham, Grendon in Northamptonshire, St. Neots in Bedfordshire, Belvoir Castle near Leicester, Southport, to mention just a few. In all cases I've found them enjoyable and worthwhile events to go to in their own right. Generally they are larger events than I experience at home. The greater numbers and standard of competition provide a big race atmosphere and a stepping stone for the scale to be encountered at championships. Travel, eating and sleeping are all aspects of the preparation for an event away from home and it is good to rehearse them. It adds to that feeling of being on a mission with a purpose. I find it imbues 'presentness', that state of being fully engaged with what you are doing, a powerful quality for getting the most out of an exercise. These are the things you can do when retired, providing some of the 'buzz' that may no longer be around as much.

Twelve
RUNNING TO FINISH

It's hot now. Within limits I'm comfortable with that; it provides something to feel, like wind or rain. It's like having company. Heat has to be respected, as I've discovered several times. When it takes its toll, the wheels really do come off. As I leave the transition zone and pass over the timing mat I'm reassured by feeling that I've reached this point, starting out on the run in the World Age Group Championships at Lausanne, and the engine still has some life in it. That was the plan.

The course takes us along the lakeside. It's flat except for two short, steep hills - steep enough for me to be reduced to a walk and to be glad of the handrail at the side of the path. But it's reassuring to notice that those around me who keep running are not moving much more quickly than I am. With hands on knees - not, I should emphasise, on hands and knees - and pushing forward, as if I had walking poles,

I make steady progress until the path levels out and I can break into a run again.

Had I known the route was taking me past the front of the Olympic Museum and that the statues to my side included Emil Zatopek and Paavo Nurmi, I might have raised a more inspirational effort. Nevertheless, the change of rhythm gives me some respite and I gain ground on some of those who had kept running. Then we are quickly back down to the lakeside for a short distance on the flat and back up and down a similar hill, though not quite as steep this time. After these interludes I'm now past halfway and it is flat once more for the remaining distance to the finish.

Of the triathlon disciplines, I find running the most difficult. It's fully load bearing and requires strength, power and spring. Since these are qualities that are affected by age, it's challenging in terms of demands on the body, in particular the legs. Having been more of a runner in the past, I am conscious of having slowed down significantly due to a combination of ageing and wear and tear.

Swimming and cycling are rhythmic; the range of movement is constant, the only variations are in tempo and in the amount of effort being applied. But because it is weight bearing, running stretches and pounds the muscles. This varies considerably according to the nature of the running surface and the extent to whether it is unyielding or cushioning, reinforcing why maintaining strength as we age is a vital component. Gradients affect the stretching of the posterior chain going uphill and test muscle resilience and 'bounce' going downhill. These factors can occur in a number of combinations in the course of a relatively short run.

Small things can be significant. Simply stepping on or off a raised kerb can cause an unwelcome jolt if not properly anticipated. If asked what is my favourite run course, I'd say without hesitation the Monikie Triathlon in Angus, which has none of these hazards. It's absolutely flat, tracing a figure of eight around two reservoirs on grassy paths and woodland trails. Without question it is the kindest course of all to the legs.

Reducing elasticity in the muscles that occurs through ageing increases the risk of strains. You can counter the effects with regular stretching and mobility exercises, as well as some plyometric (hopping, jumping, bounding) exercises. For many years I've used compression shorts for running - both when training and racing - to provide support to the hamstrings and quads. These make a big difference by holding and supporting the leg muscles, reducing the effects of muscle 'bounce' and lessening the risk of injury. The feeling of confidence they give should not be underestimated.

It took me much longer to realise the benefit of using calf guards. Opinion is divided on their use. Some say they cause muscle cramp and others swear by them. Having found them transformational, I am in the latter camp. They don't make me run any faster but they allow me to train and race with fewer problems. So while my running training remains modest, it is of a better consistency than it was a few years ago - and that has been reflected in my performance.

Normally I will run on my own so that I'm in control of how far and at what pace I am going without being influenced by what might be suitable for someone else. I'll wear a wristwatch when training to tell me how long I've been running for or to time an interval but I don't wear a watch when competing. Generally I will focus on a specific aspect of my running movement such as foot strike, upper body position or leg speed - all off road to avoid the hazards of unyielding surfaces. Some of my running is done fresh 'off-the-bike', which is a useful way of warming up as well as good preparation for races.

I have to acknowledge the benefit that core stability and balance bring to all forms of movement. When running, at least one foot is always off the ground - anything else is walking. But it's to be hoped that in fact both feet will be off the ground for a significant proportion of the time. As Anne put it to me: how can you run properly - landing on one foot, swinging the other leg through and driving forward again in good alignment - if your balance and core are weak? A point well taken, and that's why my exercises include walking lunges holding my arms above my head. Usually I find that maintaining general fitness - from swimming and cycling and from a good programme of exercises for flexibility and core stability - can offset running fitness. And when fatigued, a strong core helps to maintain form. After preparing in this way, I have found that I can usually accomplish the 5km distance in a sprint triathlon satisfactorily.

Together with Chris, I am now an enthusiastic advocate of parkrun, the weekly 5km timed runs that happen all over the country in parks near everyone. These runs cemented a breakthrough I was making in my running. I no longer thought about whether I was ready to do a parkrun, I just got up and did it. It's not about trying for personal bests each week but having a good quality run, gaining more familiarity with the 5km distance, finding my tempo and trying to hold proper form. And every now and again posting an encouraging time rewards me. From the age of 71 my running has improved. It's not necessarily become quicker but it's certainly more consistent, more comfortable and less tense. And that has added considerable enjoyment.

I have had to adapt. I am not able to run the way I did in the past with loping strides. Through regular swimming and core stability exercises, I have gained a modicum of upper body strength that was completely lacking before. As a consequence my weight has increased by a couple of kilos compared to what it was 10 years ago and I feel better for that. But the bigger change has been a general reduction of power. So now I take shorter strides but it's been very difficult to quicken the tempo and move away from drifting into driving.

Sometimes I have to modify my approach according to prevailing limitations. A common one is the hamstring tightness that's often lingering in the background and frequently in the foreground immediately after dismounting the bike. In these circumstances I try to take short quick strides to avoid over-stretching the muscle and I feel grateful for the reassurance that comes from wearing compression shorts. Troublesome ankles or insteps on the other hand will require a softer mid-foot strike.

By the time I reach the running part of a triathlon, after swimming and cycling, I am well warmed up and have become fully absorbed in the race. In that situation I often find the occasion has taken over and any issues that might compromise my running are forgotten. The event serves to banish the niggling problem - the cleansing effect I spoke of in an earlier chapter. But if there is no preliminary activity, I spend time on warm-up exercises using a roller and stret-ching routines to ensure that I have mobilised a range of movements greater than I am about to draw upon when running. There is no shortcut. It is time well spent that will reduce the risk of being sidelined.

Running regularly is key, the body becomes accustomed to it. The parkrun routine provides this for me. And it is always easier running in the company of others when the pace is right. I will try to fit in two other runs during the week, on soft surfaces, but they will be relatively short commensurate with my capability. This helps to remove the fear of risking injury from running.

I've referred to the need for the engine to have some life in it when setting out on the final part of the triathlon. For years I've experimented with numerous brands of energy bars and gels, and at various times believed I had found the best plan. But what seems fine when training does not necessarily work well in a race when the intestines have to work that bit harder.

My first experience of energy drinks was around the time of the jogging boom. Many had taken up jogging and the first thing joggers wanted to do was to run a marathon. And I didn't appear to be a credible runner if I hadn't. Eventually I decided to set matters straight by entering the first London Marathon in 1981. The Gatorade provided at aid stations was a novelty. I'd heard about Gatorade but never sampled it. I took it instead of the water on offer.

I'd also heard stories about hitting the wall but had no personal experience of it. But with a few miles still to go my stomach was churning and my legs ceased to function. The wall of encouragement for a runner in trouble was not my backdrop of choice for the remaining distance to Buckingham Palace. When I returned the following year to settle unfinished business, I took only water at the aid stations and ran in comfort the whole way to finish in a time beginning with a two. My marathon box was ticked.

In the past I favoured High-5 and Powerbar energy bars but I settled for High-5 because, when on the move, a Powerbar was too difficult to separate from its wrapper. Even if I removed the bar from the wrapper beforehand and placed it in something else it made little difference. It just clung to whatever enveloped it. Perhaps the design fault has been rectified but since moving on I wouldn't know.

During a race I no longer touch anything containing electrolyte. I leave that for afterwards. But there are still many variables with nutrition and hydration. Taking half a High-5 energy bar around halfway on the bike course appeared successful for a while, until I thought that also taking a gel towards the end of the bike ride would counter some fading towards the end of the run. However in my final year in the 65-69 age group there were several occasions when I had that hitting-the-wall feeling with more than a kilometre still to go to the finish. I was convinced that shouldn't be happening in a sprint triathlon involving not more than 90 minutes of effort. And as I would feel fine again immediately after finishing, the effect was clearly a temporary intrusion in the race effort.

That led to another experiment in my final race of the season at the Mid Argyll Triathlon when I decided to take no in-race nutrition other than sipping some water as necessary to keep hydrated. The outcome was a comfortable performance with no fading towards the finish. Perhaps energy bars and gels were the problem, not the solution. However, I failed to follow this line of thinking through fully at the beginning of the next season and didn't abandon energy bars and gels completely until mid 2017, which was about 18 months later.

Since that point I've continued a 'no nutrition water only' policy for races of up to 90 minutes, and not looked back. Now my only concession to an energy boost, which again goes back many years to orienteering days, is to consume half a Mars Bar about 40 minutes before the start, a 59g bar from a multipack (and by the way, they're only a fraction of the size they used to be!). Then, after the race, I'll finish off the other half. So many things have gone full circle from the habits and practices of the past. I've ended up reinventing what worked best for me 30 or 40 years before.

Returning to my run at World Age Group Championships - I've rounded a dead turn with about 2km still to go to the finish, back along the lakeside towards Lausanne. I am enjoying the freedom of having started the race with no limiting issues. In theory I could relax and let go. I'm in a situation where there are people ahead who might be caught if I maintain this tempo, but also others I've seen behind at the turn who look as though they are running more quickly than I am. This helps to spur me on.

At the remaining aid stations I sip some water and pour the rest over my head and shoulders.

And I do maintain my tempo right through to the blue carpet with the flags and the noise of the finish and I hear my arrival being announced. I have passed one or two runners in the final kilometre, though others will be well ahead, and finish with what speed I can muster to be sure I don't lose a place in the last few metres.

Someone is kneeling at my feet. A young girl is removing the timing chip from my left ankle. I thank her profusely; it must be the most unappealing task of all, unfastening these soggy straps while being dripped on from above. But

I am certainly in no state to bend down and do it myself. Once you reach the final 100m, with spectators on both sides and hear your name announced, it's impossible not to raise a spirited finish. This leaves you even less capable of bending down to remove the timing chip. But within moments, exhilaration takes over and exhaustion is forgotten.

I reacquaint with others I haven't seen for some time and compare notes while helping myself to bananas, watermelon and energy drinks. They call this the recovery zone but we're in the open and the sun's beating down. I spot Chris waving to me from beyond the fence and head over. It's a kilometre walk back to the transition area to collect my things from the bag drop and more walking uphill back to the hotel. Yes, my legs do feel a bit weary now.

I go online to see how I've done. 16th in my category from about 50 starters. Well satisfied. I gained five places on the run, passing six and only being overtaken by one. Being my fourth year in the 70-74 age group I reckoned that most of my opponents this time would be youngsters by comparison. As I like to point out, at the older end of the age spectrum - and certainly beyond the age of 70 - age-related advantage is more significant when measuring yourself against those in your five-year age band.

My day had started at five in the morning, setting up in transition. It's one thing to inflate your tyres in darkness but quite another to be able to read the pressure gauge on the pump - something else to learn: take a torch for very early starts. Even before daybreak the air was warm and it didn't come as a surprise when the non-wetsuit decision was announced. I was relaxed about that.

With each age group starting as a separate wave, concluding with the oldest, it was a long drawn-out process before taking to the water. The lake looked magnificent, its beautifully clear water sparkling in the bright morning sunshine. The swim course, in the shape of a shallow arc, took us to the transition zone further along the lakeside. It's always more satisfying not to return to the starting point, to feel that you've travelled somewhere. I felt confident during the swim, starting positively and settling into a comfortable position to come out of the water in the first half of my field.

The draft legal bike ride - my second experience of this following the qualifier at Redcar the year before - meant I was riding my road bike, not my TT bike. But due to the hilly nature of the course there weren't many drafting opportunities. I was either climbing at my own pace, passing others or being passed, or trying to keep well spaced on the quick descents. Travelling at more than 60kph at times, I wasn't comfortable having anyone near me. It was difficult to tell how well I was performing but I was focused on the plan, on being sensible and avoiding the spent zone. I did lose a few places to stronger riders but was satisfied that I had been riding at about the optimum to put myself in the right place for starting the run with some life still in the engine.

The whole event was such an exhilarating experience, just being there and taking part in a world championship.

But not just taking part. I also knew I'd had a good race and there wasn't really anything I might have done differently. And that's an amazing feeling. Not something you can easily describe to someone who hasn't been there.

Thirteen

END OF SEASON

It's late September, which as usual means I'm at Loch-gilphead for the MacQueen Bros Mid Argyll Triathlon. After the climax of late summer, with a world age group event in early September, it's good to have an opportunity to harness the accumulated fitness and form before bringing the season to a close. And it's also good to be taking part in one of the domestic events that are the lifeblood of our sport. The Mid Argyll race is the one I've done most often - 11 times, I calculate, at the time of writing. I keep going back because it's a real gem in a wonderful part of the country, organised by an experienced team from the local club. It's competitor focused with light touch efficiency. A favourite t-shirt of mine is the one that says "MacQueen Bros - probably the world's best removers and storers".

John calls us to the poolside a few minutes before my heat is due to start. He does a roll call and all 16 of us are present. It's a short swim in a small pool: 25 lengths of a 20m pool, 500m total instead of the usual 750m, four swimmers in each of the four lanes. Very cosy. Cosy because we've chosen to be in this heat. A couple of weeks beforehand we had all received an email containing a draft of the heat allocations and offering an opportunity to switch - either because my expected swim time may have changed, or because I'd like to be in the same heat as someone else, or indeed because I preferred not to be in the same heat as another person. That we are all starting in a contented frame of mind is a fair assumption.

The lane officials, seated on their chairs at the far end, clap and cheer as we come onto the poolside. We return the compliments by applauding them too. John introduces them and explains that they will be counting our lengths and watching the lane etiquette. He clarifies that irrespective of how many lengths we reckon to have done it is the lap counters' version of events that matters. So if we think we have completed 25 but are told to do another two we should just get over it and carry on. In such a friendly atmosphere that sounds just fine.

The lengths go past quite quickly and out of habit I count them. I find it easy to keep count if you say every second number out loud. Loud enough that you can hear yourself saying it, but not so loud as for others to hear - lest they should think you are nuts. With the previous number still ringing in your ear, you don't lose count. Reassuringly, at 23 I get a tap on the head to indicate two to go. All is well and there is nothing I have to get over. At least not yet.

The transition area is compact - two lines of bike stands and some additional rails to one side for the teams. Traditionally there are prizes for the quickest transition times, and the times achieved are astonishing. I couldn't get near them, not even if I ran through without regard to the needs for my bike ride or run. So I stick to my practised routine with no ambitions for a transition podium.

The bike course of 20km is a panhandle shape, with the handle about 2km in length, taking a clockwise route through magnificent countryside. Part of it follows the Crinan Canal that provides a significant shortcut for the sea route round the Mull of Kintyre, through locations made famous by Neil Munro in his tales of Para Handy and the Clyde puffers that plied the west coast.

In the briefing we were reminded that on the bike course there are two swing bridges crossing the canal, bridges that can open at any time to let boats through. And though unlikely, this has happened before during a race. If held up we'd just have to admire the scenery for a while and not get upset. Something else we'd just have to get over. But just imagine if it was your triathlon that paused while a puffer chugged through. You could dine out on that a few times. It does add to the anticipation, but there was no such excitement this time.

There's also usually a stiff wind to contend with. It isn't blowing too strongly this year but it's coming from the northeast, not the customary south-westerly. It also rains a lot in Argyll but today it has a gentle touch - intermittent light showers interspersed with sunshine, mild enough that we need no additional layers of clothing.

I'm not sure where I'm placed as we leave T1. Although my objective is to relax and enjoy the event I still have a race plan. I enjoy it much more if I do. My plan is to ride steadily and put effort into the two modest gradients.

The first one comes after 2km when we cross the first swing bridge and climb gradually alongside the locks at Cairnbaan to the canal's highest point. Then it's downhill and flat, into the wind over the Great Moss until we reach the main Oban road once more and head back towards Lochgilphead. The second incline comes at about 15km but again it's fairly modest and this time the wind is at our backs. Over the bike course I catch and pass four riders without anyone passing me. Psychologically that's encouraging, as is having a tail wind for the final stretch back to transition. It gives some respite to feel ready for the run.

Previously I have, rather too often, made an unnecessary meal of T2. The Mid Argyll race happens to be the location where most of these incidents have occurred. Though since it's the event I've participated in most often it could just be a statistical consequence. Regardless, right at the top of my race plan I've put a note to engage full concentration throughout the whole of T2. And as I approach transition I do just that - ensuring I rack my bike quickly and efficiently, that the shoes I'm putting on are mine and there are no stray objects inside them, and that I go round the cone at the far end and head out of the run exit, not the bike exit. All good.

The run course is 6.5km, slightly longer than the usual 5km, balancing out the shorter swim distance. I'm a little less happy this year to find they've surfaced over the grit, as I'm more comfortable on yielding ground. But the course is still one of my favourites, absolutely flat as it goes out and back along the canal path to Ardrishaig through inspiring scenery.

After a kilometre or so a runner overtakes me. I recognise him as the person who was ahead of me going into T2. That's always good, confirming the advantage gained from an efficient transition. There are runners from earlier heats coming the other way and eventually some with race numbers from my heat. As the canal meanders through picturesque countryside and the houses of Ardrishaig begin to appear, I expect to see the turn, but no, it's always beyond the bend after the next one. But because I am prepared for that realisation this time, the turn comes sooner than expected. And having turned I notice other runners from my heat not far behind, ones I'd overtaken on the bike. Before long two of them have hunted me down and given encouragement as they go past.

Others from a later heat start to come past as well. However, I maintain a steady, comfortable pace as planned and once past the boathouse there's just over 1km to go. Then it's down the ramp from the canal-side to the marshals at the main road and the final 200m to the finish gantry outside the swimming pool where there's the welcoming sight of soup, sandwiches and cake laid on by the local Scout group.

For all the races I've done in far-flung places, this local one still ranks among the highlights.

I've said that you shouldn't compare yourself with what you may have done before. It's about the present, and the satisfaction of having the best race possible in the context of how you are at the time. But having done this event regularly over a period of more than 10 years it serves as a good benchmark and later I do some analysis. This time, ignoring teams, I've finished 37th out of 101 individuals (men and women, all ages). I'm happy with that, in an open event with a spectrum of abilities.

My time is better than each of the three previous years and just a minute and a half slower than 10 years before when I was 63. My run times are getting slower but swim times have remained relatively consistent over the years and bike times have generally improved. There's high volatility in the transition times but the better ones are getting better. But certainly the overall quality of the performances has improved, showing greater consistency. And that's what is stimulating.

Both my transitions this year were respectable by my standards - 60 seconds for T1 and 47 seconds for T2, but those taking the prizes achieved 24 seconds and 14 seconds. Now that's going some! And that's the reason why you shouldn't compare yourself with what others do.

With the season finished, I'll take a break from triathlon for a few weeks - a period of R&R. In the past I've tended to take this literally and not do any swimming, cycling or running. But I actually find it unsettling not doing the things I would normally do and that I enjoy doing. So unless there are specific issues requiring rest or time to repair, I aim not to stop entirely. Instead I'll remain active according to how I feel and take the opportunity to do some different things.

I swim weekly in the lochs with a few others through September and October. The water has cooled considerably since the summer but I wear neoprene gloves and booties. In my final session of the year the water at Loch Lubnaig is the coldest it's been and the weather changes rapidly from mist to rain to sunshine - all very dramatic. As some of my companions don't wear wetsuits, I have to affect disinterest in the water temperature but I've acquired greater tolerance for cooler water. But you still have to be aware of how you are feeling and keep an eye on each other so that you're heading back to the shore before coldness penetrates.

As much as I'd like to be able to claim an open water swim in Scotland for November, I'm content to have reached as far as the clocks changing, which is six weeks beyond any previous year. The others, hardier souls than I, continue right through the winter and will no doubt be tempting me back again in the spring.

Compared with just a few years ago, there are now many more people roaming the lochs, wild swimming in rather the same way as there are those who wander the hills. Wading into a loch and swimming to the shore on the far side is a feeling of exhilaration, freedom and adventure.

And I would never have experienced this had I not been taking part in sport.

At this time of year I review the past 12 months. Kim has given me a series of questions to consider. What has been different this season? What was most enjoyable? What have I learned? Why does triathlon matter to me? What do I want to work on over the winter that will enhance the following season? I don't find out whether the answers exist until I try to write them down. The discipline of writing things down separates the wood from the trees for me, keeping a perspective on the bigger picture.

Well, what has been different? I've taken part in more events than in previous seasons. Limitations have been different - more to do with fitness and strength rather than injury issues. And my increased number of races has given me a more regular 'cleansing', with fewer opportunities for my pre-event niggles to occur.

Going a little deeper, I've come to understand better the concept of 'presentness', the state of being fully present and engaged in what I am doing, and the influence that can have on performance. In retrospect I can recognise situations where this has happened and where it has been lacking. And this year I've also gained a better understanding of momentum - the psychological momentum that can be gathered through a series of races in preparation for one that is more important. They are fascinating concepts that are refreshing to play around with; there is the luxury to do this entirely for your own enjoyment.

I need to give some thought to formulating my answers. Over the winter I should prioritise health while keeping fitness 'ticking over' so that I have a platform ready to take forward into the early season. My swimming was sharpened at the end of the year and that has given me some ideas to make a difference to my cycling, which is an area in need of attention. But perhaps that is best left until warmer weather in the spring.

Fourteen
REFLECTION

Those who support me say that age is a number not a barrier. Why should it inhibit my thoughts? And certainly, aspects of my performances continue to improve. Though I am conscious of the effects of ageing, I'm content being the age I am. My focus is simply on countering the natural trend by trying to improve technique, efficiency of movement and general performance 'know how'.

I like that I can participate with others - take part in training sessions, go wild swimming, join group bike rides - without regard to my age or theirs. On the occasions I come to participate in significant age group championships, European and World, I am competing amongst the very best. The pleasure comes from being worthy to take part in such company, not a podium contender in normal circumstances, but able to give a respectable account of myself amongst them. And that's enormously satisfying.

When I returned from the championships at Lausanne, people asked how I got on - did I win? Perhaps I should take it as a compliment. But no, I finished 16th, it was a BRP and I was delighted with my performance. I have to find ways of reducing others' expectations and say that I'm getting deep into the age group, competing against youngsters and so on. But what matters is how I feel about my performance and the vicarious pleasure I can give to my closest supporters.

If I look back to when I retired and started to pursue the sport with passion, I've taken part in around 100 events covering 17 countries and 4 continents. That's a lot of towels, t-shirts, water bottles and bananas. It's not about winning. Results come from taking part and doing your best. And every so often a performance will converge with opportunity and you can find yourself on a podium. It's the journey, not the destination.

When I went to my first international championships in 2007, seeing some of the best athletes in the world doing what they are good at made a deep impression. I was part of this sport, competing against some of the best of my contemporaries in the same setting. It was a thrilling experience and left me feeling that if this was what I could do in retirement then I would like to do more of it.

Although there followed a gap of a couple of years, I have been to at least one of the European or World Age Group Championships each year from 2010 to 2019, quite often to both. The world events are higher-profile not just for their scope but because they are normally held at the end of the season in conjunction with the World Triathlon Series Grand Final for the elite competitors.

It transports you into the fantasy world of being a full-time athlete for a few days, focused on preparing for your race. Everywhere there are individuals and groups out running and cycling. You must be careful not to get swept up in thinking you should be doing everything they are. I've learned to be more concerned with what will prepare me best for race day - checking out the bike course and cycling the run route, having a look at the swim start and swim exit arrangements but without feeling the need to practise swimming the course. I will take it easy the day before my race.

These championships have taken me to many places I would not otherwise have thought to visit, throughout Europe and further afield to Beijing, Auckland, Edmonton and Chicago - all wonderful experiences on the back of a triathlon. Usually Chris will accompany me and then go exploring while I'm engrossed in race preparation. We'll both enjoy watching the events, particularly the elite races. And often we will stay on to be tourists for at least a day or two.

The numbers of participants in European and World age group championships have increased significantly since I first started taking part. When world championships are held in Europe there is always good representation from further afield, especially from North America and the

Southern Hemisphere. So when the championships are not in Europe, I feel an obligation to try and reciprocate the effort. The presence of a good critical mass of competitors from a spread of countries enhances the occasion for everyone. And for those who do well, their achievements feel that much more rewarding.

I'm showing my age by saying that most of the t-shirts are not to my taste. Those covered in advertising, with loud messages or quirky witticisms do not appeal and the material of which some are made is poor. Those with an unintended spelling mistake are more interesting. But every now and then there is one that I could walk down the street wearing: the distinctive cut of Auckland 2012, the surprisingly tasteful one from Chicago, TriYas 2016 and the quality garments from MacQueen Bros at the Mid Argyll Triathlon. The Aberfeldy Middle Distance event has also excelled on a number of occasions. However, if the goodies were in the price, I would prefer the entry fees to be less handsome. Though medals that signify achievement - and that's a subjective measure - are appreciated, we should always be mindful of those for whom an event's completion is the fulfilment of a personal ambition - and that deserves celebration.

Reaching 70 has been the threshold for a new phase. My approach to training and racing has shifted from intensity of effort towards relaxation and flow. This has benefited my fitness and health, not trying to drive myself into the ground but seeking consistency and momentum. I have been learning continually, discovering and understanding myself and how I react in various situations.

2016, when I turned 70, was the year I shifted my focus to achieve the best bike ride to give me the best run, developing the 'flow' mindset. Swimming performances were becoming more consistent than before and I felt less inhibited by non-wetsuit swims. Using calf sleeves, recommended by fellow competitors Ron and Trace, had been a revelation. I just wish I had discovered them sooner. I was having fewer issues with pre-event niggles and managing them better. Most of the weaknesses were to do with poorly paced bike rides.

2017 was my best year to date in terms of satisfying performances and fewer physical inhibitions. I was still tinkering with in-race nutrition but had returned to the view that 'nothing is best' for a sprint triathlon - and my opinion hasn't changed. Stamina was an issue on the bike-run at times, not matching the energy applied to the early parts of the bike course. Clearly, pace judgement still needed to improve. There were things I could work on that would benefit my running but the exercise and gym programme undertaken over the winter had undoubtedly enhanced the season.

In 2018 after months of searching, I acquired some excellent replacement orthotics through podiatrist Alastair that were lighter and better than the original, discontinued ones. These were carbon-fibre devices constructed by a laboratory in Aberdeen from scans of my feet. They helped to bring greater comfort and confidence to my running, enabling me to focus on some of the other changes I needed to make.

There were other significant developments too. When not dealing with issues of extreme heat, I found it was possible to work harder on the bike without compromising my run. Wetsuit removal issues I thought had been solved proved not to have been; it was still erratic. But having seen me struggle to remove my wetsuit on one of the Thursday swims at Loch Venachar, Elspeth from the tri club passed me a can of TriSlide. It was magic, transforming the rest of the season.

New mental strength experiences were developed - momentum, its relationship with flow, and an experience of peripheral vision while being 'in the moment'. I was reminded to always prepare for adverse weather conditions, even when they seemed unlikely. That reminder prompted me to devise a shelter for protecting shoes in the transition zone that has since proved successful.

Arguably 2019, my fourth season in the 70-74 age group, has been my best and I would rank it ahead of 2017. This was mostly because of how the racing programme was managed in relation to the outcomes for priority races. I have a better understanding of the techniques I've learned and the relationships between them. Running has been much more regular, once again an enjoyable habit. I'm doing parkruns most weeks - an antidote for PEN syndrome. The exercise and gym programme was carried through more successfully by according it a higher priority in my training, to the benefit of both health and performance. Looking ahead, there is still work to be done with my cycling, with scope to introduce some of the factors that helped my swimming. A task to follow through in the spring.

On silver linings: It was only through being injured that I encountered physiotherapist Jane, whose expertise had me up and running again in my late 50s and kept me going in the period that followed. She opened the door to the specialist skills of physio Anne and it was Jane's suggestions about mental recovery that set me on the path to working with Kim. If all this hadn't occurred, I might have stopped before I was 60.

*   *   *   *   *

Times change. It's 2020, my early season in Abu Dhabi has started and I've taken part in the TriYas event in readiness for the main ITU event at the beginning of March. But the ITU World Series event doesn't happen. Sport everywhere stops. The global coronavirus pandemic is putting life for all of us on hold and the rest of the 2020 season may not even happen. The priority for older people is to look after ourselves, be safe and keep well. Looking ahead, talk is of when we 'come out the other side'. Whatever that will look like it's going to be different, another new beginning.

Appendix 1

Participation Rates in Older Age Groups at World Championships

It is a known fact that in developed countries people are living longer, which has led to more older people being physically active and taking part in sport. The main surge in participation has come from the generation of 'baby boomers' born in 1946 and the years that followed. Most participation is of a recreational nature but along with the increased interest in exercise has come an increase in participation in competitive sport where there are opportunities in both team and individual sports for older people to compete against others of a similar age, often referred to as Masters competition.

Triathlon has been part of this growth pattern, both in terms of increasing numbers of older adults who participate and those who compete in age group competition. Age group championships are held at national, European and world level. Numbers taking part have been increasing year on year.

Focusing on those who are amongst the most competitive, the following table shows numbers participating in older age groups at the world championships covering the period from 2007 to 2019.

World Age Group Championships

Participants (men and women) in Sprint and Standard distance events

		Age Categories				Total
		60-64	65-69	70-74	75-79	
2007	Hamburg GER	121	67	37	9	234
2008	Vancouver CAN	119	53	37	10	219
2009	Gold Coast AUS	143	65	25	11	244
2010	Budapest HUN	136	80	37	9	262
2011	Beijing CHN	72	43	22	6	143
2012	Auckland NZL	142	87	39	18	286
2013	London GBR	269	169	86	39	563
2014	Edmonton CAN	149	127	65	22	363
2015	Chicago USA	225	153	84	49	511
2016	Cozumel MEX	169	86	59	18	332
2017	Rotterdam NL	207	155	86	42	490
2018	Gold Coast AUS	226	183	97	43	549
2019	Lausanne SUI	271	182	131	54	638

While the location of the championships can have some bearing on the numbers participating, there is nevertheless a significant upward trend. For men and women participating in sprint and standard distance events in the four categories covering 60 to 79 years of age, it is reasonable to compare the numbers at Hamburg in 2007 (234) with those at Lausanne in 2019 (638), an increase of 173% over 12 years. The numbers in each of the four age groups have increased significantly, particularly those for categories 70-74 and 75-79. It is likely that this trend will continue.

Appendix 2

Research Findings Relating to Ageing in Sport

Research studies into performance in sport suggest that age-related decline follows a general downward curve that becomes more pronounced around 60 years of age before decreasing exponentially beyond 70. Although the gradient of the curve will vary for different sports, the more rapid decline by the age of 70 appears to be a common feature. Studies suggest that the decline in performance with age is mainly linked to a decrease in maximum aerobic power, known as VO2 max. This is the body's capacity to bring in oxygen through the lungs and transport it through the blood supply to the muscles for production of energy. Although maintaining high levels of training into older age may slow the rate of this decline, a decrease in VO2 max is inevitable.

That, along with other issues such as muscle mass, heart rates, blood volume and the capacity of the working tissues to take up and utilise oxygen, is part of an extensive canvas of the science underpinning ageing in sport. There are other factors as well that may be just as significant: levels of motivation in older athletes, attitudes to health and social benefits of participation, and changing training habits in terms of volume and intensity that in turn are affected by the longer recovery periods between training sessions and races older athletes require. And, as many older people will testify, injury prevention and management issues are often present.

A group of researchers in France, using data from the 2006 and 2007 world age group championships for Standard Distance, published a paper on age-related decline in performance in triathlon[1]. The study looked at both overall performance and performances in the individual disciplines.

A significant effect of ageing was observed on the overall performance and on performances in the individual locomotion modes, with marked differences between swimming, cycling and running. In swimming a significant decline in performance was noted after the age of 40 years. However in cycling, decline in performance was not significant until 55 years of age. A difference between the patterns of decline for cycling and running was observed only after 55 years, when running performance decreased more rapidly. This was attributed to greater muscular fatigue that is experienced during running. On the basis that cycling occupies the

---

1   Bernard, T., Sultana, F., Lepers, R., Hausswirth, C., & Brisswalter, J. (2010). Age-related decline in olympic triathlon performance: effect of locomotion mode. *Experimental aging research, 36*(1), 64–78.

greatest proportion of time during a triathlon, the greater age-related declines in performance in swimming and running beyond the age of 55 imply that swimming and running times assume a greater significance for the overall performance at the older end of the age range, particularly beyond the age of 70.

Looking at the overall picture, the study concluded that significant decline in performance with age for triathlon begins at 45 years for competitive age group athletes. This value was higher than for those they had noted for previous studies in the single sports, suggesting that alternating different locomotion modes during a triathlon may help to delay the first significant decline in performance by allowing athletes to specifically manage their physiological capabilities.

Researchers in the United States carried out a study into age-related decline in swimming and running as individual sports[2]. This study contains findings for highly trained athletes in running (10,000m) and swimming (1,500m), which are the distances in a Standard Triathlon. For running, it was established that performance over 10km is maintained until around 35 years of age, followed by modest increases in running times until 50 to 60 years of age, with progressively steeper increases in times thereafter. The analysis for swim-

---

2   Tanaka, H., & Seals, D. R. (2003). Invited Review: Dynamic exercise performance in masters athletes: insight into the effects of primary human aging on physiological functional capacity. *Journal of applied physiology (Bethesda, Md. : 1985), 95*(5), 2152–2162.

ming was taken using data from the U.S. Masters Swimming Championships, which also showed performance declining with age in a curvilinear manner. However, in swimming the reduction in performance with advancing age was smaller than that observed for running. It was also found that the age at which an exponential decline began to occur was later in swimming (about 70 years of age) compared with running (about 60 years of age). There were several reasons that could be explored as to why there should be this difference. These included biomechanical dependencies, the non-weight-bearing nature and lower incidence of orthopaedic injury during swimming compared with running, and also because interval-based training is more prevalent in swimming.

The various studies support the view that age-related changes in performance are specific to the task involved. In a triathlon the disciplines can be affected in different ways from when performed on their own. Swimming is the area most at variance with the findings from solo activities. Partly that is because it comes at the beginning of a multi-sport activity with implications for conserving energy for cycling and running that are to follow. But it is a technical sport and comparison is being made with highly trained masters swimmers, whereas swimming is the element of triathlon where older competitors tend not to be as highly skilled. In a triathlon other issues come into play, such as drafting in a group and wearing wetsuits that will have a bearing on performance. For cycling and running, there are fewer differences compared with the solo sports. That competitors are not starting from fresh but having to adapt from swimming to cycling and from cycling to running is not always fully appreciated when assessing levels of performance.

To that I would add an observation of my own. Triathlon is a relatively young sport. Older triathletes have come to the sport later in life without the substantial background in all of the three disciplines that others who have been involved from a younger age would have gained. My impression is that amongst older triathletes there is a wider divergence of skill levels across the disciplines, and this can afford opportunities for improving skills that will mitigate the general effects of age-related decline.

We have noted that age-related decline does not follow a straight line. It is a downward curve that becomes more pronounced around 60 years of age before decreasing exponentially beyond 70. This means that within a five year age category the relative age advantage for those at the younger end compared with those at the upper end becomes greater with increasing age. In championships it's not surprising to find that a preponderance of those participating are in their first and second years of an age category compared with the number in their third, fourth and fifth years. It reflects the competitive nature of the championships that those with a relative age advantage are more likely to participate.

It's a sport that offers considerable scope for further analysis.

Appendix 3

Research Findings - Swim Pacing for a Sprint Triathlon

The optimum profile for a triathlon swim differs from that for a straightforward swimming event, as the main consideration is its contribution to the overall triathlon performance. Some analyses have been carried out on the effects that different effort levels and pacing during the swim will have on the overall outcome in a sprint triathlon. One investigation examined the effect of intensity of swimming effort on subsequent cycling and overall performance[1]. It concluded that completing the swim at a maximum time trial intensity was not conducive to the ensuing discipline performances and the overall outcome. Swimming intensities of both 80% to 85% and 90% to 95% were both found to be beneficial for subsequent cycling and running times and for the overall per-

---

1   Peeling, P. D., Bishop, D. J., & Landers, G. J. (2005). Effect of swimming intensity on subsequent cycling and overall triathlon performance. *British journal of sports medicine, 39*(12), 960–964.

formance. The advice was to avoid encroaching upon an intensity exceeding 90% of maximum in order not to impair the overall triathlon performance (the term 'intensity' here was used in relation to swimming speed).

This study was taken a stage further by a group who investigated the effect that different swim-pacing profiles could have on subsequent performance in a sprint triathlon[2]. Experiments were conducted for three pacing profiles described as positive, negative and even. All three swims covered the 750m distance in the same time. The even paced swim was at a constant 82.5% of subjects' respective benchmark time trial speeds, which had been performed at maximum effort. Positive was starting fast (92% intensity) and gradually slowing the pace to finish at 73% intensity; negative starting slowly (73%) and gradually increasing the pace to finish at 92%.

Analysis of the results indicated that a faster overall triathlon performance time was achieved during the positive swim pacing exercise - i.e. starting quickly - compared with the even and negative pacing. It led to an improved cycle time that was deemed significant when compared with those for the even paced and negative paced swims, which gave similar cycling times. However there was no significant difference for the subsequent running times, which appeared to

2   Wu, S. S., Peiffer, J. J., Peeling, P., Brisswalter, J., Lau, W. Y., Nosaka, K., & Abbiss, C. R. (2016). Improvement of Sprint Triathlon Performance in Trained Athletes With Positive Swim Pacing *International journal of sports physiology and performance*, *11*(8), 1024–1028.

be unaffected. Nevertheless, the improved cycle time for the positive paced swim was reflected in the overall time for the full triathlon.

In actual races the swim tends to start at a relatively higher intensity level as competitors try to avoid congestion or seek to benefit from drafting off faster swimmers. The important lesson is to ensure there is a reduction in intensity level towards completion of the swim in order to capture the beneficial effect a positively paced swim can have for cycling performance: being able to cycle more strongly without greater effort.

Appendix 4

Event participation statistics

The author's participation in events since 2006 (age 60)

		World and European Age Group Championships			
Age Group	Year	Triathlon		Aquathlon	
		World	Euro	World	Euro
60-64	2006				
	2007	✓	✓		
	2008				
	2009				
	2010	✓			
65-69	2011	✓	✓		
	2012	✓			
	2013	✓	✓		
	2014	✓	✓		
	2015	✓	✓		
70-74	2016		✓		✓
	2017		✓		✓
	2018		✓	✓	✓
	2019	✓			✓

		All Events		
Age	Year	Triathlons	Aquathlons	Aberfeldy Team swims 1.9km
60	2006	8		1
61	2007	7		
62	2008	1		1
63	2009	1		1
64	2010	4		1
65	2011	5		1
66	2012	6		1
67	2013	10		1
68	2014	7	1	1
69	2015	8	1	1
70	2016	8	2	1
71	2017	9	2	1
72	2018	8	3	1
73	2019	10	2	

Countries (other than UK)

Austria	Germany	Spain
Canada	Hungary	Switzerland
China	New Zealand	Turkey
Denmark	Portugal	UAE
France	Slovakia	USA

Acknowledgements

I am indebted first of all to Jane Kerr, Anne Forsyth and Kim Ingleby whose professional expertise made the triathlon journey possible.

For the book itself, strategic ideas provided by Anne Forsyth and Simon Puttock allowed it to take form and Simon's critical input helped shape later drafting. Feedback on drafts was provided by Julia Hector and by friends outside of triathlon - Ron Halliday as an author and Paul Sinton-Hewitt, who has brought running into the lives of so many people. Paul's family connection with my wife Chris was discovered only because of parkrun - an example of its capacity as a force for bringing people closer together. Kim Ingleby provided support throughout, making the process from which a book emerged quite simply happen - a remarkable skill she has whatever the task in hand.

Thanks are due to copyeditor Rin Hamburgh and to Dave Perkins and Hayley Kyte from the design team at Hullo Creative. Their attention to detail and style is gratefully acknowledged. And my special thanks are extended to Alistair Brownlee for contributing the foreword.

Most of all I wish to thank my wife Chris for encouraging and supporting me the whole way and being the one whose suggestions were real game changers.

Any unattributed photographic images were taken by Chris or myself.

Born in Edinburgh in 1946, Douglas Wood has always been a runner. A former orienteering Scottish champion, he represented GB and later managed the GB team at the World Orienteering Championships.

A mathematician by training, he followed a career in university administration before retiring in 2007 and pursuing his passion for triathlon, taking part in events all over the world while coaching at his local club in Stirling.

Since retiring Douglas has won Scottish Age Group titles in triathlon and aquathlon and has represented GB in European and World Age Group Championships on many occasions. In 2012 he received the 'Master Sportsperson of the Year' award from Stirling Sports Council.

Away from sport he is a keen photographer, enjoys travel and exploring, and appreciates art and good music. His love of the Scottish hills and wild places led him to complete the 'Munros', climbing every peak in Scotland over 3,000 feet.

Douglas and his wife Chris live in Stirling. They have three children and three grandchildren.

Lightning Source UK Ltd.
Milton Keynes UK
UKHW020745231120
373894UK00003B/10

9 780993 536687